TO

_____

FROM

_____

DATE

_____

100 DAYS TO

DREAM YOUR HEART OUT

A Devotional Journal

KATY FULTS

DaySpring

LIVE YOUR FAITH

CONTENTS

Dream Your Heart Out

Everyone's talking about dreaming these days. There are cute wall hangings in every store with bold, bright colors reminding you to dream big. To outdream yourself. That your dream is achievable. And even to *Dream Your Heart Out*. Doesn't it sound so exciting? Like you just want to throw caution to the wind, pursue your passions, and always live like the sky is the limit. Sometimes God-given dreams are placed in your heart and they ignite a fire in you that becomes relentless. It takes a lot of trust in the Lord and a lot of confidence in Him to remember that He can do immeasurably more than you could ever imagine or dream of in your life. God can't wait to align your desires to His when you trust in Him with all of your heart!

So let us come boldly to the throne of our gracious God.
There we will receive His mercy,
and we will find grace to help us when we need it most.
HEBREWS 4:16 NLT

Now glory be to God, who by His mighty power
at work within us is able to do far more
than we would ever dare to ask or even dream of—
infinitely beyond our highest prayers,
desires, thoughts, or hopes.
EPHESIANS 3:20 TLB

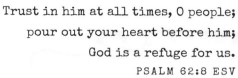

Trust in him at all times, O people;
pour out your heart before him;
God is a refuge for us.
PSALM 62:8 ESV

pRayer

Lord, help me to trust You
with my deepest dreams and greatest passions.
I surrender them now to You.

A Hope And A Future

Do you have a passionate desire for your life that you long for, pray for, and dream about? Maybe you want to get married, maybe you want to start a family, maybe you want to start a business or find a new job. It can be a difficult process to trust in the Lord that He has a perfect plan ready for you, but once we surrender our lives, hearts, and dreams to Him, it becomes so freeing to be able to live our lives to the fullest, waiting in anticipation to see how the Lord works His perfect plan out. The Lord plans to give us a hope and a future. And while there are times that it is more difficult than others to wait for that and trust in Him, the best thing to do is to trust that He has your best interests and heart in mind.

Therefore I tell you,
whatever you ask for in prayer,
believe that you have received it,
and it will be yours.
MARK 11:24 NIV

When doubts filled my mind,
Your comfort gave me renewed hope and cheer.
PSALM 94:19 NLT

DAY

2

I praise God for what He has promised.
I trust in God, so why should I be afraid?

PSALM 56:4 NLT

Prayer

Lord, I pray today that You will continue
to reveal Your plan to me and
give me strength as I trust in You.

Dare To Dream

Have you ever dared to dream something that felt impossible or completely out of your reach? On one hand it can feel like the most exciting thing you've ever hoped for, and on the other hand it can be the scariest thing you've ever done. The good news is that there is no dream that is too big for God to make happen. He delights in giving us more than we could ever dream or imagine! He is passionate about lavishing love on His children and giving us the desires of our hearts as we trust in Him. When you feel like your fears are taking over, make sure that your faith outweighs them. Remember to put your hope in God instead of your plans and your dreams. Trust in His perfect plan for your life and your journey.

For nothing will be impossible with God.
LUKE 1:37 ESV

What no eye has seen, nor ear heard,
nor the heart of man imagined,
what God has prepared for those who love him.
I CORINTHIANS 2:9 ESV

DAY

For the LORD is good;
his steadfast love endures forever,
and his faithfulness to all generations.

PSALM 100:5 ESV

PRAYER

Lord, help me feel Your love in times
where it's more difficult to trust
in Your perfect plan.

Wait For His Plan

It's risky for us to release our own plans and desires we have for our lives and the control we're holding onto and surrender them to the Lord, trusting that He is going to take care of us. If we are handing over a part of our lives that is scary, if can oftentimes feel like worry and dread are taking over. Here's the deal though: I don't think God wants that for us. I think He wants us to wait for His plan to be revealed in His own timing with anticipation and excitement for the future. When we release control and trust in the perfection of His plan, we are realizing and acknowledging that He is going to work everything out for His glory and our own good. And because of this, He will fill our hearts with more joy than we could ever imagine!

Wait for the LORD;
be strong, and let your heart take courage;
wait for the LORD!
PSALM 27:14 ESV

I will instruct you and teach you
in the way you should go.
PSALM 32:8 NIV

DAY

Those who listen to instruction will prosper;
those who trust the Lord will be joyful.

PROVERBS 16:20 NLT

Lord, guard my heart from worry as I wait
for You to reveal Your plan for my future.
Fill my heart with joy today.

God Has Not Forgotten You.

Are you anticipating something and it's just not happening as quickly as you'd like? Sometimes the wait can be excruciating and take more time than we were expecting. And it's so hard to be patient and trust that we are still on the right path and that God is still directing us. We grow weary and discouraged, and we want to take matters into our own hands. Be encouraged, though. God has not forgotten you. Your name is engraved on His hands. Your dreams are in the forefront of His mind. It might not always be easy, but if you can let go of the way you want it to all work out and trust that His ways are higher than yours, you will be able to experience His peace that transcends all of your understanding.

See, I have written your name
on the palms of My hands.
ISAIAH 49:16 NLT

Teach these new disciples to obey
all the commands I have given you.
And be sure of this: I am with you always,
even to the end of the age.
MATTHEW 28:20 NLT

DAY 5

When doubts filled my mind,
Your comfort gave me renewed hope and cheer.

PSALM 94:19 NLT

Prayer

God, I give it all to You.
I don't want to be in control of my life;
I want You to take it. Fill me with Your heart
and lead me where You want me to go. I'm Yours.

Go In Peace

There are a lot of stories in the Bible about how Jesus performed a miracle and healed people because of their faith. It's always inspiring to me to read the stories behind these miracles. One that comes to mind is the woman in Luke 8. This woman was bleeding for twelve years without any way of being healed. Think about how long she waited for an answer, how long she waited to feel better. She was out of options, but she believed that if she could just touch the corner of Jesus' cloak, she'd be healed. She believed it with all her heart and so she did it. And you know what happened? When she finally touched Jesus' cloak, He turned to her and said, "Your faith has made you well. Go in peace" (Luke 8:48 NLT). When we believe with all our hearts that Jesus will meet our needs and provide for us, we will be on the receiving end of miracles.

But blessed are those who trust in the Lord
and have made the Lord their hope and confidence.
JEREMIAH 17:7 NLT

And he said to her,
"Daughter, your faith has made you well;
go in peace."
LUKE 8:48 ESV

But if we must keep trusting God
for something that hasn't happened yet,
it teaches us to wait patiently and confidently.

ROMANS 8:25 TLB

PRAYER

Jesus, thank You for meeting my needs and
providing for me, even when I don't see it yet.
Thank You for strengthening my faith.

He Binds Up Our Wounds

Have you ever wanted something so badly that you've prayed for it with all your might? You've dreamed huge, prayed bigger, and you've had faith that it will happen. Maybe you've waited years, maybe you've put your blood, sweat, and tears into it. You've believed with your heart and soul that it will happen....and then it doesn't. Now what? You have a broken heart and your dreams are crushed. Believing this is the way God wants it to be may seem impossible, and the feeling of having to start over may seem overwhelming. Listen, though: God's Word says that He draws near to the brokenhearted. He binds up their wounds. When everything you've hoped and prayed for doesn't happen the way you thought it would, rest your weary heart and know that God is drawing you close to Him and He is not abandoning your dreams. He is holding your heart close to His.

The Lord is close to those
whose hearts are breaking;
He rescues those who are humbly sorry
for their sins.
PSALM 34:18 TLB

He heals the brokenhearted,
binding up their wounds.
PSALM 147:3 TLB

DAY 7

Let Him have all your worries and cares,
for He is always thinking about you and
watching everything that concerns you.

I PETER 5:7 TLB

pRayer

God, I am hurting today. Please comfort me
and allow me to feel Your presence.
I know that You are drawing me in close.

Overcoming Comparison

Sometimes it can feel like everyone else in life is getting what you want. You want a baby so badly and everyone around you is getting pregnant, except you. You want to get married and everyone around you is getting engaged, except you. You want your dream job and everyone's getting hired, except you. And during these times, it's easy to let your thoughts run wild with jealousy. You start thinking horrible things like *She doesn't deserve the life she has,* or *He only got that job because of his family,* or *Their marriage will never last.*

Yes, jealousy can creep in and overtake us when we don't even realize it. When this happens, though, we can lean on God and talk openly to Him about our negative thoughts. We can ask Him to take the jealousy away and fill us with gratitude instead. With God, we can defeat jealousy and envy by focusing on the path God has for us and trusting His plan for our futures.

Love is patient, love is kind.
It does not envy, it does not boast, it is not proud.
I CORINTHIANS 13:4 NIV

Do nothing out of selfish ambition or conceit,
but in humility consider others as
more important than yourselves.
PHILIPPIANS 2:3 CSB

DAY

8

A tranquil heart is life to the body,
but passion is rottenness to the bones.
PROVERBS 14:30 NASB

Prayer

God, please remove any jealous thoughts
from my mind and replace them with gratitude.
You've done so much for me, Jesus, and I love You.

LIVE FOR TODAY

There might be a lot of anticipation and excitement for the days ahead of you, but God has given you only one today. He gave you today with brand-new mercies waiting for you when you woke up. He gave you today with new chances to give Him the glory, new chances to extend grace and kindness to others, new chances to follow hard after God and His heart. You have one sunrise today and one sunset. Will you slow down enough to savor them? The pull to dwell on all that you're waiting for will be strong, but you have this one chance to enjoy this day. To make the most of the opportunities given to you today and to enjoy the blessings God has laid in front of you. What are some ways that you can invest in your today? What are some things you can do to glorify the Lord with these next twenty-four hours?

The thief's purpose is to steal, kill and destroy.
My purpose is to give life in all its fullness.
JOHN 10:10 TLB

Give your entire attention
to what God is doing right now,
and don't get worked up about
what may or may not happen tomorrow.
God will help you deal with whatever hard things
come up when the time comes.
MATTHEW 6:34 THE MESSAGE

DAY 9

Teach us to realize the brevity of life,
so that we may grow in wisdom.

PSALM 90:12 NLT

PRAYER

Lord, thank You for today.
Help me to glorify You with it.
Help me to live this day to its fullest
and to take joy in all my circumstances.

Pray Your Heart Out

What is it that you're dreaming about? What is it that you're praying your heart out over? Is it to find reconciliation in a broken relationship? Is it that your children will come to know Jesus and His saving grace? Maybe it is that you'll get married one day or start a new business adventure. Don't give up and don't stop praying about it. Pray with all your heart! Pray that God will open your eyes to the ways He is showing up for you and speaking into your heart in the process. He is providing for you in ways you don't even see yet! And in this time, remember that God is not leaving your side. He is growing you into a person of endurance and character. Keep praying your heart out and keep your eyes fixed on Jesus.

And we are confident that He hears us
whenever we ask for anything that pleases Him.
I JOHN 5:14 NLT

I pray that your hearts will be flooded with light
so that you can see something of the future
He has called you to share.
I want you to realize that God has been made rich
because we who are Christ's have been given to Him!
EPHESIANS 1:18 TLB

DAY

I call upon you,
for you will answer me, O God;
incline your ear to me; hear my words.
PSALM 17:6 ESV

pRayer

Lord, open my eyes to the ways You are showing up for me.
Give me clarity in my next steps.
Help me to know that I'm walking the path
You laid out for me.

Unforeseen Plans

You wake up when your alarm goes off and you have your entire day planned out down to the minute. Your to-do list is synced up and ready to go with boxes that are begging to be checked off. You can almost hear the "Eye of the Tiger" music on repeat in your brain as you set out to tackle the day ahead of you. And then the inevitable happens...something doesn't go as planned. A sick kid calls from school. A meeting goes too long. The grocery store doesn't have what you need. Now what? Do you let disappointment take over and ruin your day? Or do you keep going and stay positive? This is how life works. We set out with our plans, our hopes, our dreams....and inevitably somewhere along the way, something doesn't go the way we thought it would. The good news is this though: God knew all along. And sometimes when our plans go wrong, He allows beautiful, wonderful, unforeseen things to happen that we were least expecting. Put your hope in the Lord and don't give up. He has a beautiful plan for you.

The heart of man plans his way,
but the Lord establishes his steps.
PROVERBS 16:9 ESV

I will instruct you (says the Lord)
and guide you along the best pathway for your life;
I will advise you and watch your progress.
PSALM 32:8 TLB

DAY 11

He has made everything beautiful in its time.
Also, he has put eternity into man's heart,
yet so that he cannot find out what
God has done from the beginning to the end.
ECCLESIASTES 3:11 ESV

Prayer

Lord, when my day has gone much differently
than I was expecting it to, teach me to surrender to You.
Remind me often that You have a beautiful plan for my life.

Letting go

Have you ever wanted something so badly in your life that you can feel your knuckles turning white over how hard you're holding onto it? As you look at your life as a whole, it's hard to imagine that any other way than what you're wanting could be right for you. But consider this: *there is so much beauty in letting go.* God has a plan. And it might look different than yours. The Bible says, "Trust in the LORD with all your heart, and lean not on your own understanding; in all your ways acknowledge Him, and He shall direct your paths" (Proverbs 3:5–6 NKJV). When we choose to let go of what we're holding onto in our lives, and instead trust in the Lord with every ounce of our hearts, He will give us the strength to walk in His way, even if it looks different than our own. We cannot begin to understand what paths God has in store for us, but when we let go of our grip on our own plan, we surrender and we set our hearts free to allow God to guide us in His plan instead.

And we know that for those who love God
all things work together for good,
for those who are called according to his purpose.
ROMANS 8:28 ESV

This God—his way is perfect; the word of the LORD proves true;
he is a shield for all those who take refuge in him.
PSALM 18:30 ESV

I will strengthen you, I will help you,
I will uphold you with my righteous right hand.

ISAIAH 41:10 ESV

PRAYER

Lord, help me release my grip on life.
Free me of anything holding me back
from pursuing Your goals for my life.

God Knows You

A garden doesn't just grow overnight. The seeds are planted in dirt. And then watered nonstop. The garden needs fertilizer and sunlight and space to grow. It needs time. Sometimes a lot of it. And it can be a long wait before you see the growth, but when you do finally see it, the wait was worth it. That dirt, that water, that space, and that time were all part of the garden's process of growth.

You've been praying your heart out and guess what? God hears every single prayer. He sees your heart, He hears your desires, and He *knows* you. He knows you. He is taking those prayers and turning them into something beautiful. He's taking His time and making sure everything in you is growing at the exact pace it's supposed to. And someday really soon, you're going to see those prayers answered and you're going to realize that waiting on God's plan was all worth it.

> But if anyone loves God,
> he is known by God.
> I CORINTHIANS 8:3 ESV

> So neither he who plants nor he who waters is anything,
> but only God who gives the growth.
> I CORINTHIANS 3:7 ESV

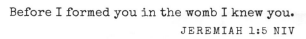

Before I formed you in the womb I knew you.

JEREMIAH 1:5 NIV

prayer

God, when I start to feel like
You're not hearing my prayers,
gently remind me that I'm fully known by You.

Keep Going

Some days you're going to wake up and have this energy that makes you want to chase your dreams and follow your heart and run so fast and so hard after your passions. You're going to gain momentum, you're going to put your hope in God, and you're going to laugh without fear of the future (Proverbs 31:25). Those are the days that give you the confidence to keep going, to keep persevering.

And other days, you're going to wake up and realize that sometimes life is just about putting one foot in front of the other. Maybe nothing feels easy and all you can do is just keep going. You just keep taking deep breaths and hope that you can make it to the end of the day and then crash down into your bed. Those are the days that are building your character to give you the perseverance you need. Those are the days you cry out to the Lord to sustain you, to hold you, to just help you get through it. You need those days so you learn to not give up. You need those days to know that God is not leaving your side.

But you, take courage!
Do not let your hands be weak,
for your work shall be rewarded.
II CHRONICLES 15:7 ESV

Though they stumble, they will never fall,
for the Lord holds them by the hand.
PSALM 37:24 NLT

From the end of the earth I call to you
when my heart is faint.
Lead me to the rock
that is higher than I.
PSALM 61:2 ESV

Prayer

Jesus, today does not feel like an easy day.
Give me strength to just keep going.
Thank You for sustaining me.

give It Your All

Dreams don't work unless we do. They won't just happen on their own. You don't just come up with an idea to start your own business and then the next day it happens. Or hope that your children know the Gospel without having to teach them about it. No, that's not what happens at all. You have to work with all your heart and your mind and your soul to obtain those dreams. Colossians 3:23 (NLT) says, "Work willingly at whatever you do, as though you were working for the Lord rather than for people." When you wake up in the morning, set your mind that everything you choose to do with that day, you do for the Lord, and not for others around you. And work with all your might for Him, knowing that He is right there with you. Whatever you do, commit your work to the Lord, not anyone around you.

Work willingly at whatever you do,
as though you were working for the Lord
rather than for people.
COLOSSIANS 3:23 NLT

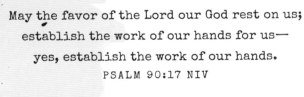

May the favor of the Lord our God rest on us;
establish the work of our hands for us—
yes, establish the work of our hands.
PSALM 90:17 NIV

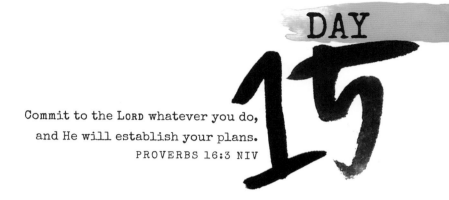

DAY 15

Commit to the LORD whatever you do,
and He will establish your plans.

PROVERBS 16:3 NIV

PRAYER

Jesus, use my mind, my hands,
and my heart to do Your work today.
I offer them all to You, Lord.

Take A Deep Breath

You know that quote, "When one door closes, another one opens"? It's supposed to bring us hope in a time of disappointment. To give us hope that just because what we wanted didn't happen, there will still be something new to come our way. It's a good reminder. But sometimes it's also good to just feel the disappointment for a little bit. Because if you've worked really hard for something and it doesn't happen, that hurts. God has the best plan for your life, but that doesn't mean that it's not hard when your plan and His don't align. So it's okay to take a deep breath and just feel the disappointment over having to let go of something you wanted. Feel what you need to feel. Give yourself time. And then, when the hurt starts to subside, allow yourself to get excited about a fresh start.

Let us hold fast the confession of our hope
without wavering, for he who promised is faithful.
HEBREWS 10:23 ESV

O Lord, You alone are my hope;
I've trusted You from childhood.
PSALM 71:5 TLB

Blessed is he whose help is the God of Jacob,
whose hope is in the Lord his God.

PSALM 146:5 ESV

PRayeR

When I feel disappointed, Jesus,
give me hope for the future You have in store for me.
I know that You will meet me here.

Dreaming A New Dream

Today is a great day to wake up and leave yesterday's disappointments behind and start fresh. Your dreams might have been crushed and your plans might have been changed and you've allowed yourself the space and time you need to grieve what you thought would be. But today is brand-new. And you are waking up to a fresh start. A fresh path ahead with no bumps in the road yet. You have a chance to pursue something new, to dream a new dream. Turn to the Lord and pray that He will align your desires with His, that He will make your heart in tune with His. It is His delight when we pursue Him with everything in us—this is your chance to start fresh with that! Believe that the Lord will reveal to you His plan when it is meant to be revealed. There is so much joy waiting for you ahead.

Seek the Lord while he may be found;
call upon him while he is near.
ISAIAH 55:6 ESV

For I'm going to do a brand-new thing.
See, I have already begun! Don't you see it?
ISAIAH 43:19 TLB

And though you started with little,
you will end with much.

JOB 8:7 NLT

Prayer

God, it is a new day with a fresh start.
Thank You for Your mercies that are new every day.

The Wait Is Worth It

There is truth to the old saying, "A watched pot never boils." It's so boring! It seems to take so long! And what a waste of time to just stand there watching when you could be doing anything else with your time in those minutes.

It's a lot like waiting for answers from the Lord. It can feel exhausting and confusing *and long.* It can feel like it's taking forever for God's plan to be revealed and for answers to come. Here's the choice though: You can stay in the same place and waste your life and let the days tick by. *Or,* you can come alive in the waiting. You can use this season to grow, to draw closer to the Lord, to allow Him to build your character. You can turn your face to Him, open up your heart to Him, and allow Him to breathe life into you during this waiting process. It isn't easy, but it's worth it. How can you come alive in the waiting today?

But you must not forget this one thing, dear friends:
A day is like a thousand years to the Lord,
and a thousand years is like a day.
II PETER 3:8 NLT

For the Lord is faithful to His promises.
Blessed are all those who wait for Him to help them.
ISAIAH 30:18 TLB

Lead me in your truth and teach me,
for you are the God of my salvation;
for you I wait all the day long.
PSALM 25:5 ESV

PRAYER

Jesus, I want to grow closer to You in this time of waiting.
I'm praying that I'll come alive in this process today.

FAITH BIGGER THAN FEAR

Today, let your faith be bigger than your fears. We oftentimes pray timidly. We're scared to pray big because what if we end up disappointed, or what if what we want is different than what God wants? Why don't you try something new today? Take the timid prayers and turn them into something loud and something bold. Don't just pray about what you think is possible. Pray for what you think is *impossible*. And pray hard about it unashamedly. And believe with your entire heart that God is going to take those impossible prayers and show you that NOTHING is impossible with Him. Absolutely nothing. He says it in His Word. So we need to believe that as truth and believe in God's power and perfect plan. Pray big and pray expectantly that God is going to show up in a mighty way.

For we walk by faith, not by sight.
II CORINTHIANS 5:7 ESV

For I cried to him and He answered me!
He freed me from all my fears.
PSALM 34:4 TLB

The earnest prayer of
a righteous person has great power
and produces wonderful results.
JAMES 5:16 NLT

pRayer

God, I believe in the power of praying boldly,
believing You can do anything.
Help me let my faith be bigger than my fears.

Following Jesus

When Jesus asked the disciples to follow Him, He didn't give them much more to work with than just that...to *follow Him*. There were no plans after that. No outline or agenda about what the next steps were. At first the men came up with excuses. But Jesus kept saying, "No, I just want you to follow Me." He wanted them to realize that whatever He had in store for the future was so much better than what they were leaving behind. He would take care of them. He wouldn't leave them stranded. And one day they would understand.

It's still like this when we choose to follow Jesus and the oftentimes unknown path He is leading us on. It's scary to leave behind what we think is the best way for us. But as we follow hard after Him, He is reminding us that He's taking care of us. He's not leaving us stranded. He's showing us that what He has in store for us is so much better than what we left behind.

Jesus spoke to the people once more and said,
"I am the light of the world. If you follow Me, you won't have to walk
in darkness, because you will have the light that leads to life."
JOHN 8:12 NLT

The steps of good men are directed by the Lord.
He delights in each step they take.
PSALM 37:23 TLB

Walk straight down the road GOD commands
so that you'll have a good life
and live a long time in the land
that you're about to possess.
DEUTERONOMY 5:33 THE MESSAGE

Prayer

Jesus, I want to learn to follow You
even when I don't know where You're taking me.
Thank You for not leaving me stranded.

When God Says No

We all have different passions and dreams. Some of us dream about our careers, some of us dream about being married or having children. Some of us dream about restoration in a relationship or being cancer free. Everyone has something that is driving them. Something they're praying for, something they're passionate about. But what happens when God says no? What happens when you don't get what you want? You have to remember God is not going to lead you into the valley and then leave you there. He is going to get you through the heartache and the broken dream. Psalm 23:4 (NLT) says, "Even when I walk *through* the darkest valley, I will not be afraid, for You are close beside me" (emphasis added). He will pick you up in the place where you're broken and disappointed and carry you through to the other side. He is faithful like that. Watch and see.

Nor height nor depth, nor anything else in all creation,
will be able to separate us from the love of God
in Christ Jesus our Lord.
ROMANS 8:39 ESV

I will not leave you comfortless:
I will come to you.
JOHN 14:18 KJV

DAY 21

Put your trust in the LORD.
PSALM 4:5 ESV

prayer

Lord, it is so hard to feel this disappointed.
Thank You for carrying me through the valley.

We Keep Growing

Have you ever bought a bouquet of tulips? Chances are, if you have, you've probably cut the bottoms and put them into water. Have you ever noticed, though, that even though they've been cut, bundled, and sold, they still keep growing? Crazy, right?! They can grow up to an inch in the vase. An inch! And not only that, but they move around while in the vase. They gracefully twist and turn and bend, all while searching for a source of light. When they've found the light, that is when they open and bloom.

I think we are just like tulips! There are times when we will be cut down, but this is when we keep growing. We will twist and turn and dance through every season. But as long as we keep searching for the Source of light, we will be able to bloom in this place, even if it's not where we thought we would be.

Your word is a lamp to my feet
and a light to my path.
PSALM 119:105 ESV

The light shines in the darkness,
and the darkness can never extinguish it.
JOHN 1:5 NLT

Light is sweet;
how pleasant to see a new day dawning.
ECCLESIASTES 11:7 NLT

PRAYER

Thank You, Jesus,
for always lighting the way for me.
Help me to keep searching for You.

Keep Singing

There are going to be really great days when you sing the worship songs in church at the top of your lungs. With excitement, with adoration, and with hopeful joy. Where you smile at the words and dance to the beat and throw your arms up in the air with wild abandonment. You may have this feeling like life is just so amazing at the moment, you feel like you could box it up and wrap it with a bow.

Some days, though, you're going to sing those same worship songs with tears in your eyes and an ache in your heart. The lyrics will be the same, but they'll take on new meaning. You'll sing about how God's a good Father and about how He's the King of your heart, and it will prove harder for you to believe those words in those moments.

Contrary to what it may seem, God understands those feelings. He understands your heartache and your heaviness. And He's meeting you in that place—when your hands are still held high but tears have replaced the exuberant smiles. Keep singing to Him and don't stop. Keep letting your feet dance even through disappointment. In the happy moments when life feels pretty great, and in the hard moments when you're just putting one foot in front of the other, He'll meet you in both places.

He is your praise. He is your God, who has done for you these great
and terrifying things that your eyes have seen.
DEUTERONOMY 10:21 ESV

Worship the LORD with gladness.
Come before Him, singing with joy.
PSALM 100:2 NLT

But as for me, I will sing each morning
about Your power and mercy.
For You have been my high tower of refuge,
a place of safety in the day of my distress.
PSALM 59:16 TLB

Prayer

God, I will praise You with hopeful joy
and I will praise You with an aching heart.
Thank You for meeting me in both places.

Growth Is A Process

The process of a caterpillar turning into a butterfly has always been fascinating. The fact that God planned for a little furry, crawly bug to create a cocoon, live in it while shedding old body parts and growing new ones, and then come out of the cocoon with beautiful wings is unbelievable. And while we may have all heard the cliché comparisons to our growth process as humans, there is truth in them. A caterpillar doesn't just wake up one day as a butterfly. It's a complex process with multiple stages and layers, and it all takes time. Just like our growth process as humans. Don't get discouraged with the journey God is taking you on right now. Embrace it and know that when God has finished shaping you in this season, you will be stronger and more inwardly beautiful than you were before.

Therefore, if anyone is in Christ,
he is a new creation.
The old has passed away; behold,
the new has come.
II CORINTHIANS 5:17 ESV

And I will give you a new heart—
I will give you new and right desires—
and put a new spirit within you.
EZEKIEL 36:26 TLB

DAY 24

And the one sitting on the throne said,
"See, I am making all things new!"
REVELATION 21:5 TLB

PRAYER

Thank You, Jesus, that You are continually giving us
strength and making us new again.
Help me to stay encouraged on the journey.

Prepare For Game Day

Have you ever played team sports? If so, you probably had weekly practices where you ran drills, strengthened your abilities, and prepared for when it mattered the most—game day. But what if you went to every practice and then when it came time to play the game, you decided not to? It would make no sense, right? The truth is: even when we spend years preparing our hearts and minds, standing on God's promises, and practicing His love, we can still decide to give up and walk away when the going gets tough. We can even make ourselves believe that it's easier to throw in the towel than to walk with God. However, when we are faced with life's obstacles, it's important to hold on to God with all we have, remembering that He is an almighty Father who is able to pull us out of the pain. Only then do we have a fighting chance at peace, only then do we have a sure way of winning in the long run.

But as for you, be strong and do not give up,
for your work will be rewarded.
II CHRONICLES 15:7 NIV

And let us not grow weary of doing good,
for in due season we will reap,
if we do not give up.
GALATIANS 6:9 ESV

Be alert, stand firm in the faith,
be courageous, be strong.
I CORINTHIANS 16:13 CSB

Prayer

Lord, thank You for staying with me through
the ups and downs of life. Help me to continue to
lean on You no matter what life throws my way.

You've got This

You've hit a wall. You've been working so hard and suddenly you've plateaued. Your goal seemed super obtainable and now it seems out of reach. It's discouraging and exhausting. And probably a little bit disappointing. But you know what? This is not the end for you. It may be hard to regain momentum and to trust that the Lord has got you taken care of. But you still have the rest of today to start fresh. And tomorrow will be brand-new! In those moments where you are confused and tired of being in limbo, take a deep breath and keep trying. And remember to trust in the Lord that He's got you. He's always with you. He will never leave you. He is strengthening you while you're at this wall. He's using it to build character in you. As hard as it may be, use this time to build your faith in Him. It may be hard, but it will be worth it. You've got this!

This is the day that the Lord has made;
let us rejoice and be glad in it.
PSALM 118:24 ESV

Let me see Your kindness to me in the morning,
for I am trusting You.
Show me where to walk,
for my prayer is sincere.
PSALM 143:8 TLB

Strength and dignity are her clothing,
and she laughs at the time to come.
PROVERBS 31:25 ESV

Prayer

Lord, refresh my soul today.
Help me to see my obstacles the way You see them.
Strengthen me, Lord. I love you.

God Is Not In A Hurry

You've got your day ahead planned out perfectly. Down to the minute.
You've got your agenda planner all synced up, and the months and year
ahead are filling up quickly. You've got it all figured out—how everything
is going to run smoothly—and you're constantly getting everything in
order and your ducks in a row. And then God says, *Wait on Me.* He says,
My plan is not your plan, and My ways are not your ways. And you're
forced to realize that God is not in a hurry. It is okay for us to have our
own plans as long as we're prepared for God to throw us a curveball and
ask us to slow down, surrender, and wait. But the good news is: in Isaiah
40 it says that those who wait for the Lord will renew their strength. So
when your agenda may not go exactly the way you perfectly planned it,
take a deep breath and remember that God is not in a hurry and that He
is strengthening you through this process. You'll be so glad that you did.

This plan of mine is not what you would work out,
neither are my thoughts the same as yours!
ISAIAH 55:8 TLB

But these things I plan won't happen right away.
Slowly, steadily, surely, the time approaches
when the vision will be fulfilled.
If it seems slow, do not despair,
for these things will surely come to pass.
Just be patient! They will not be overdue a single day!
HABAKKUK 2:3 TLB

They who wait for the LORD
shall renew their strength;
they shall mount up with wings like eagles;
they shall run and not be weary;
they shall walk and not faint.
ISAIAH 40:31 ESV

PRAYER

God, when I am in a hurry, and You are not,
give me the patience to wait for Your perfect timing.
Renew my strength every day.

Running After God's Own Heart

Have you ever thought about King David's life? Like *really* thought about it? He was called as the future king of Israel when he was a young boy. Started ruling the nation at age thirty. He had an affair with a married woman. Got her pregnant. In order to cover up his sin, he had her husband murdered. And yet, he was called "a man after God's own heart." Crazy, right? But if we take a deeper look at his life, we learn that he sought after the Lord with his whole heart. He ran after God's heart. He lived a life of faith, of repentance, of thankfulness, of obedience. He pursued the Lord with everything in him and because of that, he found favor with God. When we run after God's heart, He runs after ours. He meets us, lavishes love on us, and pours His grace and mercy on us. David messed up, but he made it right and pursued God in a way that we should follow after. It's not too late to make that your story too.

> But seek first the kingdom of God and his righteousness,
> and all these things will be added to you.
> MATTHEW 6:33 ESV

> But from there you will seek the LORD your God
> and you will find him, if you search after him
> with all your heart and with all your soul.
> DEUTERONOMY 4:29 ESV

I sing to God, the Praise-Lofty,
and find myself safe and saved.
PSALM 18:3 THE MESSAGE

PRAYER

God, thank You for pursuing me so well
with Your love as I learn to better seek You.
Thank You for running after my heart.

God Has Big Dreams For You

Life can be completely disappointing sometimes. We think, hope, pray it's going to go one way and instead it goes in a totally different direction. There are tears, confusion, and unanswered questions. And suddenly there's a lack of control because the future is out of our hands. This is where we have to let go. We have to let go of what we thought this season would look like, this year, this life. This is where trust comes in.

We have to surrender our dreams and our desires and trust in God's plan, even when it doesn't look like our own. We have to remember that God is just. He is not going to plan out a life for us that we can't handle. He loves us. He dreams with us. He is also trustworthy. Let go of the disappointments when the plans you desperately wanted don't work out, and trust that God has your best interests and your best dreams in mind.

> Humble yourselves before the Lord,
> and He will lift you up.
> JAMES 4:10 NIV

> Be still, and know that I am God.
> PSALM 46:10 ESV

DAY 29

Trust in the LORD with all your heart,
and do not lean on your own understanding.
In all your ways acknowledge him,
and he will make straight your paths.

PROVERBS 3:5-6 ESV

Prayer

Jesus, thank You for sitting with me in my disappointment.
I completely trust You with my future.
Help me see where to go next.

Jesus Is The Only Way

If you've ever seen someone in the beginning stages of cancer, they may look like everything is completely normal, since cancer is an internal disease. They can carry on as usual before symptoms start showing and no one is able to tell that there is a life-altering illness wreaking havoc on their body. They might even feel okay in the beginning stages, and it may seem like it's not going to drastically affect them. But without treatment, the cancer will invade their organs and will interfere with body functions that are necessary to live. It will eventually lead to death.

This is also how it works with our hearts when they aren't aligned with God's Word and His heart. When we choose to walk in darkness instead of the Light, everything can look perfect on the outside, but on the inside it is slowly breaking us down. We need Jesus. We need His truth and we need His grace and we need His redemption as treatment. And we need to surrender our will and our desires and align our hearts with His. He is the only way.

You can't whitewash your sins and get by with it;
you find mercy by admitting and leaving them.
PROVERBS 28:13 THE MESSAGE

Then if My people will humble themselves and pray, and search for Me,
and turn from their wicked ways,
I will hear them from heaven and forgive their sins
and heal their land.
II CHRONICLES 7:14 TLB

His life is the light that shines
through the darkness—
and the darkness can never extinguish it.
JOHN 1:5 TLB

prayer

Jesus, shine Your Light on the dark areas
of my heart today and pour Your grace over the areas
that need Your forgiveness and redemption.

Bring Someone In

Sometimes, when you are in a season of waiting for God's answers and God's timing, it can feel lonely and isolating. It can be difficult to figure out how to relate to people who aren't experiencing the same feelings that you're experiencing. It can feel scary to be vulnerable and open about what you're going through. But people want to be brought in. They want to know how to show up, and if you push through the scary part, you'll see the body of Christ come alongside you. Whether it's walking through disappointments and crying with you or dreaming with you while you dream a new dream, people want to know how they can walk through life with you. If you're feeling isolated and lonely and this waiting period is hard on you, how can you bring someone in today?

So encourage each other
and build each other up,
just as you are already doing.
I THESSALONIANS 5:11 NLT

The heartfelt counsel of a friend
is as sweet as perfume and incense.
PROVERBS 27:9 NLT

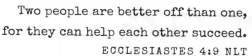

DAY 31

Two people are better off than one,
for they can help each other succeed.

ECCLESIASTES 4:9 NLT

prayer

I praise You, God,
for the friendships You bring my way
and that point me back to You.

Saying Yes Today

Have you ever used or heard that phrase "I woke up on the wrong side of the bed"? You woke up irritable and grumpy for no particular reason. You feel like saying *no* to everything. It's easy to feel stuck there, especially if things just aren't going your way. You have a choice at those times. You can stay on that side of the bed for the rest of the day, or you can choose to start saying *yes*. You can say yes to starting over. Yes to blooming and growing. Yes to the unknowns of the day. Yes to surrendering to Jesus today. Yes to praising Him even when you don't always feel like it. You can say yes to loving yourself, loving others, and loving God today. And say yes to shining His light today. Say yes to serving someone else. And say yes to going the extra mile. Your day will change, and you will be so happy you chose to live it well.

Create in me a clean heart, O God,
and renew a right spirit within me.
PSALM 51:10 ESV

Above all, fear the Lord and
worship Him faithfully with all your heart;
consider the great things He has done for you.
I SAMUEL 12:24 HCSB

Then I lay down and slept
in peace and woke up safely,
for the Lord was watching over me.
PSALM 3:5 TLB

Prayer

Lord, today is Your day.
I'm choosing to say YES to You today, Jesus.
Point me in the direction of Your will.

Jesus Is The Master Designer

If you've ever sought out to paint a room, you know that there is a lot more work that goes into that project than just painting. You have to purchase the supplies, clean up the room, move the furniture away from the walls. You have to tape off the areas of the room that you want to protect, like ceilings, baseboards, and window frames. Then you paint the first coat and you wait for it to dry before painting the second coat and sometimes even the third. The quicker you go, the more mistakes you can make, and the sloppier it can get. It's best to take your time.

Jesus is the master designer of our lives. And He's careful with how He creates. He takes His time with us, making sure He gets it just right. Are you putting Him on a deadline and rushing Him? Or are you giving Him time to mold you in His perfect timing? If He's making you wait for something, be patient. He is doing something extraordinary.

Better to be patient than powerful;
better to have self-control than to conquer a city.
PROVERBS 16:32 NLT

What no eye has seen, nor ear heard,
nor the heart of man imagined,
what God has prepared for those who love him.
I CORINTHIANS 2:9 ESV

I am the Lord, the God of all mankind;
is there anything too hard for Me?
JEREMIAH 32:27 TLB

PRAYER

You have designed my life perfectly and carefully.
Lord, give me the patience I need
to wait for You to reveal Your plan.

Making The Most Of Today

Waiting is oftentimes very hard. Say you go to a doctor's appointment. You get there to check in fifteen minutes before your appointment, like they advise you to do, only to wait. And wait. And wait. So annoying! So you have to find something to do when you're there. You catch up on social media on your phone, read all the outdated magazines in the lobby, zone out to the daytime talk show on the television. You realize you should have brought something more productive to do while you wait: work, a book, a scarf you're knitting. At least you could have made the best of it.

If God has you in a season of waiting right now, it might be easy to waste time sitting around—discouraged, frustrated, disappointed with the time He's taking on you. But you have a choice! You can let it get the best of you, or you can get the best of it. Live your life to the absolute fullest every day and give God the glory for all He is doing in your life, even during these days that seem like they're dragging. Make the most of where you're at right now! It will be worth it.

And let us not get tired of doing what is right,
for after a while we will reap a harvest of blessing
if we don't get discouraged and give up.
GALATIANS 6:9 TLB

Cast your burden on the LORD,
and he will sustain you.
PSALM 55:22 ESV

DAY 34

Therefore, whether you eat or drink,
or whatever you do,
do everything for God's glory.
I CORINTHIANS 10:31 HCSB

pRayeR

God, thank You for every little thing
You've done for me lately.
Help me to turn my frustration into gratitude
during this season of waiting.

Your Story Is Not Over

So you've dreamed your heart out. And you've worked your hardest. And at the end of the day, things just didn't work out the way you thought they would. You feel like you've failed. And there's embarrassment and discouragement. It's hard not to dwell on all that went wrong. But take a deep breath and pause for a few minutes. And recognize all that God did in your life and in your heart during this time. Think about the things He taught you, the ways He grew you, and the new lessons He shared with you. This season was not wasted, and your story is not over. There is about to be a brand-new beginning and a change on the horizon. And everything you've walked through up until now—the good and the bad, the progress and the failures—God is working it out for your good.

My flesh and my heart may fail,
but God is the strength of my heart,
my portion forever.
PSALM 73:26 HCSB

The godly may trip seven times,
but they will get up again.
PROVERBS 24:16 NLT

DAY
35

My grace is sufficient for you,
for my power is made perfect in weakness.
II CORINTHIANS 12:9 ESV

Prayer

Lord, my plan failed but I know Yours doesn't.
Help me see the ways You have used me even in this season.

THE LORD WILL FIGHT FOR YOU

There are a lot of days when you will wake up and you'll feel strong and capable and like you've got this. You can conquer this. But there are other days when you will feel the weight of the world on you. When you don't feel strong enough and you don't feel capable enough. When everything just feels heavy and like a battle you're not ready for. But remember that you don't need to carry this on your own. You don't need to fight this on your own. The Lord will fight for you. He says in Exodus 14:14 (ESV), "The Lord will fight for you, and you have only to be silent." So take a deep breath and be encouraged. This battle does not fall on your shoulders. God is taking over, calming your soul and your fears and lightening your load. Be still. Be refreshed. Let Him fight for you.

For the Lord your God is going with you!
He will fight for you against your enemies,
and He will give you the victory!
DEUTERONOMY 20:4 TLB

If God is for us,
who can ever be against us?
ROMANS 8:31 NLT

The LORD your God fights for you.
DEUTERONOMY 3:22 HCSB

PRAYER

Lord, You promise to go before me and fight for me.
I will be still and trust in You.

When God Changes Your Dream

Sometimes God changes your dreams. You've worked really hard. You've prayed even harder. You've thought all along that this is what God wants for you. But what if it's not? Think about your passion, your dream, your prayer. Maybe you are desperate for a baby of your own. Maybe you have a deep desire to get married. Maybe you want to see reconciliation in a broken relationship. Those are all big, huge dreams that take trust and courage and dedication. But what if God takes your dream and changes it? And what if—deep breath—it's better than you could have ever imagined it to be? What if he says no to that baby of your own and says yes to adoption? And what if you realize that is what was meant for your life—to adopt children who had no family of their own? We have no idea on this very day what God is planning for tomorrow, but we need to be able to live in a way that is open to what He has in store for us. It will be bigger and better than we could ever dream or imagine.

Be still, and know that I am God.
PSALM 46:10 ESV

Let the peace of heart that comes from Christ
be always present in your hearts and lives,
for this is your responsibility
and privilege as members of His body.
And always be thankful.
COLOSSIANS 3:15 TLB

From His abundance we have all received
one gracious blessing after another.

JOHN 1:16 NLT

prayer

Lord, I may not understand the path
You are taking me on right now, but I know that
You work all things out for my good and Your glory.
I'm excited to see what You are doing.

A Place Of Healing

Sometimes God says no to your dream. It's not that He's changing it or surprising you with a new one, it's just that He is saying, "No, that's not what I am planning for you." He's not doing it to be mean or unkind. He's doing it because He knows what is ahead, and what is ahead doesn't match up with what you are praying and hoping for. He's calling you to trust Him, even in the midst of heartbreak and disappointment. He's saying, "Listen, My child. I know your heart is hurting and there are a lot of unknowns. And you might be angry and hurt. But trust Me that I know the plans I have for you. I will not abandon you, and I will give you a future full of hope." It is okay to be disappointed when God says no. It is okay to hurt and to cry big, huge tears. But take those feelings, open up your hands, and give them to God. He knows how it feels and He's ready to walk with you to a place of healing.

Lord, how long will You stand there, doing nothing?
Act now and rescue me,
for I have but one life and these young lions are out to get it.
PSALM 35:17 TLB

GOD, my God, I yelled for help
and You put me together.
PSALM 30:2 THE MESSAGE

O Lᴏʀᴅ, how long will You forget me? Forever?
How long will You look the other way?
How long must I struggle with anguish in my soul,
with sorrow in my heart every day?
PSALM 13:1-2 NLT

Prayer

God, I am hurting and angry right now
but I know You will not abandon me.
I know You have a plan for my future
and that is what I'm trusting in.

God Is Still Growing You

Did you know that God grows potatoes underground? Like, *way* underground. They are planted six to eight inches down in the ground and they need a lot of space to grow. They need to be planted at least two feet away from the next potato. They grow in dark, unseen places and take several weeks before you can see any fruition. But once they're done growing and ready to be uprooted, they're ready *right* away and should be enjoyed the first day they're dug up.

If you're in a dark place similar to the potato, take heart. God is still growing you. He's doing hundreds of things in your life that remain unseen. And someday soon, He's going to be finished with this growth process and you'll be able to see the fruit come to life. You'll be able to realize and understand all that He's been doing under the surface and you'll be able to put it to use right away.

The good thing about potatoes is that they're sometimes turned into french fries. And who doesn't love a good french fry?!

For we are glad when we are weak and you are strong.
Your restoration is what we pray for.
II CORINTHIANS 13:9 ESV

For God is working in you,
giving you the desire
and the power to do what pleases Him.
PHILIPPIANS 2:13 NLT

For when the way is rough,
your patience has a chance to grow.

JAMES 1:3 TLB

prayer

I know You are using this time to grow me, God.
I may not understand it right now, but I will someday soon.
I pray You continue to strengthen my faith.

Keep On Praising Him

The weather can often dictate our moods. If it is bright and sunshiny, we tend to feel the same. Happy, content, with a pep in our step. If there is a storm brewing outside, we may feel stormy in our hearts. Cloudy, gray, and gloomy. It's hard to say why the skies affect our moods so much, but one thing is for sure: we need to keep praising Him under every sky. When the skies are blue, we praise Him. When the skies are gray, we keep praising Him. When we choose to look up with hopeful eyes, we can be sure that God sees us. He sees us in times of beauty, in times of ease, in times of chaos and heartache. We can be sure of that. We can be sure that on this day, no matter what shade of blue or gray the sky is, we are being guided to the exact place God wants us to be. So keep on holding on to hope and keep on praising Him no matter what sky you feel like you're under today. He is not leaving your side.

O LORD, you are my God;
I will exalt you; I will praise your name,
for you have done wonderful things,
plans formed of old, faithful and sure.
ISAIAH 25:1 ESV

Let every living, breathing creature praise GOD!
Hallelujah!
PSALM 150:6 THE MESSAGE

DAY 40

All day long I'll praise and honor You, O God,
for all that You have done for me.

PSALM 71:8 TLB

pRayer

Jesus, no matter what the sky looks like today,
I'm going to choose to praise You for all
You have done and are doing in my life.
Thank You for sticking by me.

Surprise!

Have you ever planned a surprise party? It's thrilling! You have this big secret and you're excited to do something special for someone you love. You put tons of details into the planning and you keep thinking, *I can't wait for them to know everything!* Because if they only knew what was waiting for them very soon, they would not be able to contain their excitement. And when you finally get to say, "Surprise!" all your hard work is paid off by their expression and smiles.

This is what Jesus says in John 13:7 (ESV): "What I am doing you do not understand now, but afterward you will understand." We should live in anticipation of what Jesus is doing in us and for us. We may not understand it right now or have a clue of what to expect, but we can trust and have faith that He is doing something we cannot even fathom yet! And when you finally get to hear from Jesus, "Surprise! This is what I've been doing for you," you'll *finally* understand.

> But I will watch for the LORD;
> I will wait confidently for God,
> who will save me. My God will hear me.
> MICAH 7:7 GNT

> All living things look hopefully to You,
> and You give them food when they need it.
> PSALM 145:15 GNT

Jesus replied, "You don't understand now
why I am doing it; some day you will.
JOHN 13:7 TLB

DAY
41

Prayer

God, I don't know what You're working on right now,
but I do know that You do not abandon Your children,
so I will anticipate Your plan with joy.

Open Your Hands

Whatever passion it is that is setting your soul on fire right now, God wants you to hold onto it with open hands. Not just to live with your dreams surrendered to Him but to actually invite Him in to your deepest desires. God wants you to be willing to dream passionately, loudly, wildly *with* Him. He wants you to trust Him with the deepest desires of your heart. To believe that He has your best interests in mind, no matter what the outcome. God wants you to never stop praying. To bring Him in every step of the way knowing that He loves you and He wants you to love Him. To talk to Him and confide in Him. And mostly, God wants you to love Him more than you love your dream. So think about it today. How can you bring God into today? How can you open up your hands and your heart to Him?

Let your hope keep you joyful,
be patient in your troubles, and pray at all times.
ROMANS 12:12 GNT

I lift up my eyes to the hills.
From where does my help come?
My help comes from the LORD,
who made heaven and earth.
PSALM 121:1-2 ESV

Always keep on praying.
I THESSALONIANS 5:17 TLB

prayer

Jesus, I want to live out my passions for Your glory!
Teach me how to love You more through them.

Be gentle WITH YourSelf

Did something happen that left you disappointed and discouraged? Maybe you got an answer you weren't expecting. Maybe something is taking longer than you anticipated. Maybe it feels like good things are happening to everyone around you and they're not happening to you. It's frustrating and disheartening and you're doing everything you can to keep your head up. Remember, though—it is okay to be angry. It is okay to feel all your feelings. Maybe it's time to talk to God about it—about your anger, your pain, your frustration. Have you called out to Him? After all, He can take it. He's not surprised, and He will put you back on the right path. This season will not last forever, and soon you will experience the frustration and anger starting to fade. Hold on to that hope! Be gentle with yourself.

Devote yourselves to prayer;
stay alert in it with thanksgiving.
COLOSSIANS 4:2 CSB

Trust in the LORD with all your heart
and lean not on your own understanding.
PROVERBS 3:5 NIV

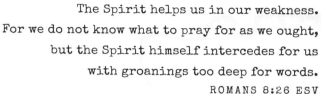

The Spirit helps us in our weakness.
For we do not know what to pray for as we ought,
but the Spirit himself intercedes for us
with groanings too deep for words.

ROMANS 8:26 ESV

PRayeR

Jesus, I'm tired and frustrated.
I can't seem to fix the situation in front of me,
so I'm asking You to take it from here.

Press On

There's so much more that goes into running a marathon than just running it. You train for weeks. You map the course—where you will run fast, where you will slow down, where you will take a bathroom or water break. You plan your music out. You eat the right foods the night before. You get a lot of sleep and rest. And when the race comes, the number-one thing to remember is to pace yourself. Every single book and article and trainer will tell you to start slow and steady. Save your energy for the moments when it matters most. And then when it's time, you give it your all. You go into the race knowing you will have moments where you will feel like giving up, but you don't. You press on, push yourself, and persevere.

When following Jesus and your dreams, do the same. Plan. Map the course. Train hard. Pace yourself, and give it your all. Don't give up. And whatever you do, press on and persevere. He is running right alongside you.

I have fought the good fight,
I have finished the race, I have kept the faith.
II TIMOTHY 4:7 ESV

Let us run with determination
the race that lies before us.
HEBREWS 12:1 GNT

I will pursue Your commands,
for You expand my understanding.
PSALM 119:32 NLT

Prayer

Jesus, I know You are with me.
Help me to run after You and Your plan with all my might,
pressing on and not giving up.

Hold on to His Promises

Following Jesus and surrendering your life to Him isn't always going to be easy. In fact, a lot of days it will be a lot harder than you ever thought it would be. There will be a lot of bumpy roads that you will travel on, a lot of twists and curves that you weren't anticipating. A lot of unknowns, a lot of valleys, a lot of mountains to climb. Faith in those moments isn't always easy, and you may have periods of time where you doubt. But God has never broken any of His promises. So when He says He will be your strength, He means it. When He says He will walk through the fire for you, He will do just that. He has never left you, and He has never not loved you. So when the path gets a little bumpier than you're used to and you're experiencing doubt, hold onto His promises to get you through. What are some truths you can remember today?

He gives power to the tired and worn out,
and strength to the weak.
ISAIAH 40:29 TLB

Whatever is true, whatever is honorable,
whatever is just, whatever is pure, whatever is lovely,
whatever is commendable, if there is any excellence,
if there is anything worthy of praise,
think about these things.
PHILIPPIANS 4:8 ESV

DAY

45

Jesus Christ is the same
yesterday, today, and forever.
HEBREWS 13:8 TLB

prayer

Lord, there are a lot of unknowns right now,
but You are always constant and always the same.
I will choose to surrender to You
even when things don't feel very easy.

Trust and Learn

We don't have to be taught how to worry or be anxious. Our hearts are good at that. We don't need lessons on how to be overwhelmed or stressed; we don't need to read how-to books about discouragement. We know exactly how to hold on tightly to our plans and our desires. These things come natural for us.

What we do need to be taught is how to be calm. How to be still. How to take our dreams and our plans and loosen our tight grip on them. We have to be taught to hand those things over to the Lord and we have to be taught to trust that He's holding them for us. These things don't come as natural for us. The amazing part of this, though, is that God is such a gentle and loving teacher. He will gently take us on a sweet journey to learn how to surrender to Him. He is patient with us and kind to us, and He will continue teaching us how these good things can become what is natural for us. Let go and allow yourself to learn from God.

Do not be anxious about anything,
but in everything by prayer and supplication with thanksgiving
let your requests be made known to God.
PHILIPPIANS 4:6 ESV

And this righteousness will bring peace.
Yes, it will bring quietness and confidence forever.
ISAIAH 32:17 NLT

He calms the storm and stills the waves.
PSALM 107:29 TLB

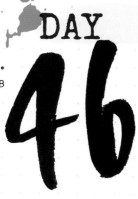

DAY
46

pRayer

Lord, when I'm anxious and worried,
teach me how to be calm and still.
Teach me how to loosen my grip on my own will
and surrender my dreams to You.

He Sees You

When you're sitting in a restaurant and the walls start to close in on you from anxiety, don't forget that God sees you. When you wake up at three in the morning and can't sleep because your heart is broken and the tears won't stop streaming, God sees you. When you feel like your life is messy, complicated, and sometimes embarrassing, remember that God still sees you. When it feels a little bit like maybe no one *else* sees you, maybe no one *else* cares, God is there. He sees you. God isn't surprised by anything you are walking through right now. He cares about you, He cares about your worries, your concerns, your grief, and your heartache. He is walking with you and holding your hand, saying, "I know you. I love you. I see you." Let it wash over you like His mercies do every morning. You are known. You are loved. You are seen.

What's more, I am with you,
and I will protect you wherever you go.
GENESIS 28:15 NLT

The LORD Himself watches over you!
The LORD stands beside you as your protective shade.
PSALM 121:5 NLT

DAY 47

O Lord, You have examined my heart
and know everything about me.

PSALM 139:1 TLB

Prayer

Jesus, help me to feel Your love
in a special way today.
Open my eyes to Your beauty
and fill my heart with Your peace.

He Knows Your Name

Is there something in nature that takes your breath away? A sunset with pink skies, snow-covered mountaintops or foam-covered seas? It's oftentimes mind-blowing to look at God's creation and try to understand that the same God who created the vastness of the ocean created you. The same God who created the highest mountain will sit with you in the lowest valley. He pursues you, chases after you, pours His love daily over you.

The same God who created this earth, this universe—who is bigger than your mind could ever fathom—looks at you in your strongest moments and your weakest moments and says gently to you, "You're known." Your name is written on the palm of His hand. He knows the number of hairs on your head. He knows your dreams. He knows your good days and your bad days. And most of all, He knows your heart. You're known.

He knows the number of hairs on your head!
Never fear, you are far more valuable to Him
than a whole flock of sparrows.
LUKE 12:7 TLB

He knows us far better than we know ourselves,
knows our pregnant condition, and keeps us present before God.
That's why we can be so sure that every detail
in our lives of love for God is worked into something good.
ROMANS 8:27 THE MESSAGE

You know when I sit or stand.
When far away You know my every thought.

PSALM 139:2 TLB

PRAYER

Thank You, Jesus, for knowing
every little intricate piece of my heart.
Thank You for chasing after me.

Teeter-Totter Through Life

Do you remember playing on teeter-totters when you were a little kid? You sat on one end and your friend sat on the other end. And as one end went up, the other end went down, and it was a never-ending source of entertainment. The thing is, though, once someone gets off a teeter-totter, it no longer functions. It only works with two people, and if you're alone on it, you're stuck. You can't go anywhere.

Sometimes life can feel like God jumped off the teeter-totter and you're just sitting there by yourself. It felt like you had a balance and a rhythm and that everything was going smoothly, and then suddenly you just *feel alone*. Remember, though, God didn't leave you. He's always there, always working, even if you can't see Him or feel Him. Sometimes we have periods of life when we don't understand what He's doing and we feel confused and lonely. Like we're sitting on one side of a teeter-totter waiting for Him to jump back on. But here's the deal: faith is believing that God is *still there* even when our sight is limited and we can't see Him. How can you find God today in your circumstances?

O God, be not far from me;
O my God, make haste to help me!
PSALM 71:12 ESV

God is our shelter and strength,
always ready to help in times of trouble.
PSALM 46:1 GNT

Then I pray to you, O Lord.
I say, "You are my place of refuge.
You are all I really want in life."
PSALM 142:5 NLT

prayer

I confess, Lord, that some days it's hard to know
what You're up to and where You are. Strengthen
my faith as You show me Your presence.

Pockets Of Beauty And Grace

Waiting for God's plan and God's timing can oftentimes feel *hard*. You just want answers and to hear His voice, but you have no idea when that will happen. But what if today you chose to look at it differently? What if—for just today—you decided to live in excited amazement at what God could possibly be doing? Take a step back from the discouragement and the discontentment from your circumstances and decide to look at this season with different eyes. Be encouraged! Look at your life and find pockets of beauty and grace that you forgot God placed there. Hold on to those! Let them wash over you with new mercy as you continue to turn to Him. Don't give up, don't hold back, don't stop finding the little joys God is still bringing your way even in your circumstances. Yes, this waiting period may feel long, but His timing and His plan will be perfect for you in the end. How can you find ways to be excited and amazed at what God is doing today?

Sing a new song to the Lord telling about His mighty deeds!
For He has won a mighty victory
by His power and holiness.
PSALM 98:1 TLB

There's no one quite like You among the gods, O Lord,
and nothing to compare with Your works.
PSALM 86:10 THE MESSAGE

God thunders wondrously with his voice;
he does great things that we cannot comprehend.

JOB 37:5 ESV

Prayer

I praise You, Lord, because You have done and
are doing great things in this season of my life.
You are faithful and I trust You.

The Happiest Place On Earth

Have you ever been to Disneyland? It's "the happiest place on earth." There's this excited energy when you walk in and everybody has the same sort of pep in their step. There are beautiful flowers, twinkle lights everywhere, colorful balloons filling the sky. It's *magical*. There are also crowds, long lines with grumpy bystanders, crying kids who are missing their naps. Somehow, though, at the end of the day, most people leave happy. Your legs hurt, you're exhausted from going for it all day, and your ears are buzzing from all the noise. But you have that Disneyland joy on your face and it's oftentimes very contagious.

As you're going through your days, as you're living out your dreams, you may be wondering why it's not always easy and not always happy. It's not always twinkle lights and balloon-filled skies. But it's a good reminder to keep the pep in your step and keep finding God in those moments. And at the end of the day, keep finding joy—it's contagious.

I have told you these things
so that you will be filled with My joy.
Yes, your joy will overflow!
JOHN 15:11 NLT

You have let me experience the joys of life
and the exquisite pleasures
of Your own eternal presence.
PSALM 16:11 TLB

Rejoice in the Lord always.
I will say it again: Rejoice!
PHILIPPIANS 4:4 HCSB

prayer

God, if today gets crazy and things don't go as planned,
I pray I still find a contagious joy in my circumstances.

It's Time!

It's time. It's time to take those God-given dreams that have been stirring in your heart and run hard after them. It's time to dream *big* and it's also time to pray *even bigger*. It's time to place those dreams in His hand and know that He has been eagerly awaiting this. God's been waiting to answer your prayers, to fulfill these dreams in His way and His plan. It's time to trust Him. To trust that His dream for your precious life is bigger than any dream you could possibly have in your heart for yourself. It's time to believe that God has your dreams and your passions in the palm of His hand. And while there may be moments of waiting, of disappointment, of closed doors and heartache, there will also be moments of immense joy. Answered prayers. Provision and constant reminders of God's love for you. Believe that you haven't seen anything yet. God is about to do amazing things for you and through you.

Trust GOD from the bottom of your heart;
don't try to figure out everything on your own.
Listen for GOD's voice in everything you do, everywhere you go;
He's the one who will keep you on track.
PROVERBS 3:5-6 THE MESSAGE

Do not be conformed to this world,
but be transformed by the renewal of your mind.
ROMANS 12:2 ESV

If you remain in Me and My words remain in you,
then you will ask for anything you wish,
and you shall have it.

JOHN 15:7 GNT

PRayer

God, I'm so thankful for all You're doing my life.
I believe You are doing amazing things and I trust in You.

Going For It

Sometimes dreaming big about something is about being patient. About waiting on God's timing. It's about seeking God's will and desire for your life and about trusting Him and growing your faith. Sometimes dreaming big causes heartache and disappointment. Failing and getting back up again. But *sometimes* dreaming big is about going for it. It's about throwing caution to the wind, surrendering everything to the Lord, and going for it with everything in you. It's about working hard, pushing yourself, and pursuing your passions for the sake of the Gospel, no matter what comes your way. Sometimes dreaming big is about saying that everything you have to walk through to get to the other side is going to be worth it to be able to bring God glory through your journey. He's using this time to strengthen you, to grow you, and to continually make you new. So how can you go for it today?

But as for you, be strong and courageous,
for your work will be rewarded.
II CHRONICLES 15:7 NLT

Put God in charge of your work,
then what you've planned will take place.
PROVERBS 16:3 THE MESSAGE

He has told you, O man, what is good;
and what does the LORD require of you
but to do justice, and to love kindness,
and to walk humbly with your God?
MICAH 6:8 ESV

DAY
113

Prayer

Lord, I place my dreams in Your hands
and I surrender them to You.
And I'm going to go for them
with everything in me!

He Fills Your Voids

Today: If you're waiting. If you're lonely. If you're hurting or grieving. If you're depressed or anxious. If you're confused at God's plan. If you feel like giving up. Consider this: You are loved by a God who thinks you're amazing. He calls you beautiful. He knows your heart so intricately. He planned your life out with a hope for your future. He feels your heartache and your pain. He wants to carry your depression and your anxiety. He wants to calm your confusion. He wants to walk with you when you feel like giving up. You are loved by a God who *sees* you. He is your comfort when things feel uncertain. He is your peace in the midst of chaos. He holds your hand when you feel lonely. And He fills the voids in your heart when things feel empty. You have a God who created you in His image.

You are absolutely beautiful, my darling.
SONG OF SOLOMON 4:7 HCSB

The LORD said, "I will go with you,
and I will give you victory."
EXODUS 33:14 GNT

I have said these things to you,
that in me you may have peace.
In the world you will have tribulation.
But take heart; I have overcome the world.

JOHN 16:33 ESV

PRayer

God, when things feel confusing, chaotic, and lonely,
thank You for filling the voids in my heart.

THIS IS WHERE WE LEARN

Have you ever had a day that started out amazing and by the end was just an absolute train wreck? You had so much hope in the beginning, and by the end you crashed into bed with defeat. It's hard to step back and watch the extreme difference throughout the day of things going smoothly and then in a moment everything falling apart. But this is where we learn to find strength in God. This is where we learn to turn to Him the minute we start to see things crumble. We learn to put our hope in Him—that He will be with us in the best parts of the day and also the worst. This is where we learn to surrender. To let go of what we dreamed of and hand it all over to Jesus. To open up our hands and release control, trusting that He will take care of us. And this is where we learn to have peace—peace that we don't understand, peace that guards our minds, peace that can only come from Jesus Himself.

Now may the God of hope fill you with all joy
and peace as you believe in Him so that you may overflow
with hope by the power of the Holy Spirit.
ROMANS 15:13 HCSB

But the LORD takes pleasure in those who fear him,
in those who hope in his steadfast love.
PSALM 147:11 ESV

DAY

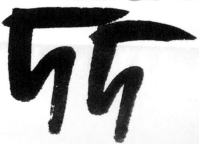

Try to live in peace
even if you must run after it
to catch and hold it!
I PETER 3:11 TLB

prayer

My mind is flooded with anxiety today, Jesus.
Calm me down with Your peace
that guards my mind.

TRUST

Trusting God is a journey. I think we sometimes wish and hope that it was as easy as snapping our fingers, but it's not. But that's the beauty of it! The times that cause us to doubt are the times that are going to produce growth and faith. You may have days where you feel uncertain and maybe you're questioning everything. Questioning if you're headed in the right direction, if the Lord is still on your side, if you should be trying more or if you should be more still. In those moments, find God's grace. It's still right there, washing over you. Find His strength. It's still right there, growing you into who He wants you to be. This is a good season for you. It's teaching you to be a better version of yourself for the next season.

But I trust in Your unfailing love.
I will rejoice because You have rescued me.
PSALM 13:5 NLT

Lord Almighty,
how happy are those who trust in You!
PSALM 84:12 GNT

Oh, give thanks to the Lord,
for He is so good!
For His loving-kindness is forever.

PSALM 118:29 TLB

Prayer

Jesus, as I'm walking this journey,
teach me how to trust in You—
in the good times AND in the bad times.
Make me a better version of myself for You.

A Whole Year Wiser

If you feel discouraged today and like you're at a standstill in your faith, in your walk with God, or in the mundane day-to-day things, think back to where you were a year ago. You are a whole year older and a whole year wiser. You had no idea a year ago that you would walk through the things you've walked through this year. You may not be where you wanted to be or where you feel like you should be, but you're so much further along than where you were. Be encouraged by this. God is growing you still in this place. He's not always quick with His lessons; sometimes He likes to take His time. So today, take a deep breath. Look back at all He's done and find peace with where He has you right now. And be excited for where He's taking you!

Yes, be patient. And take courage,
for the coming of the Lord is near.
JAMES 5:8 TLB

But grow in the grace and knowledge
of our Lord and Savior Jesus Christ.
To Him be the glory both now and to the day of eternity.
II PETER 3:18 CSB

DAY 57

So then, just as you received Christ Jesus as Lord,
continue to live your lives in Him,
rooted and built up in Him,
strengthened in the faith as you were taught,
and overflowing with thankfulness.
COLOSSIANS 2:6-7 NIV

prayer

God, thank You for sticking with me this past year.
Celebrate with me today as I reminisce on
how far we've come on my faith journey.
I can't wait to see where You take me next.

Diving Right In

Have you ever stood on the edge of a pool, knowing the water was going to be pretty cold but also knowing that you were going to have to eventually jump in? You have this inner monologue with yourself over whether or not you should go for it. Sometimes you even talk yourself into believing it is so much colder than it actually is. But you know it has to be done, so you take a deep breath and dive in. Sure, it's chilly at first. But then after a few seconds, your body adjusts to the temperature, and you realize you're glad you did it.

Maybe you're standing on the edge of something in your life and you know you have a decision to make. You know you can either stay on this ledge, looking at what lies ahead and letting the fear of the unknown control you, or you can dive right in. You can take a deep breath and jump into the uncertainties and the unknowns, trusting that God is going to be holding your hand and guiding you. You might not need to plug your nose for this jump, but you definitely need to keep praying.

You need to keep on patiently doing God's will if you want Him
to do for you all that He has promised.
HEBREWS 10:36 TLB

We humans keep brainstorming options and plans,
but GOD's purpose prevails.
PROVERBS 19:21 THE MESSAGE

He said to them, "Because of your little faith.
For truly, I say to you, if you have faith like
a grain of mustard seed, you will say to this
mountain, 'Move from here to there,' and it will
move, and nothing will be impossible for you."

MATTHEW 17:20 ESV

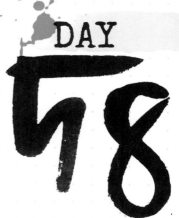

DAY 58

pRayer

God, I am taking a deep breath
and jumping into uncertainties.
I know You will not leave my side.

A Fresh Start

We all have a past. No one is exempt from that. Some of us have pasts that are pretty tame, and some of us have pasts that are wild. No matter what, though, we all have things we can look back on and regret. We all have areas of life where we wish we would have followed Jesus harder. Our pasts and regrets can oftentimes weigh us down and hinder us from moving forward. But that's the most amazing thing about the Gospel. The Gospel says, "I'm taking your past, your regrets, your poor choices, and your heaviness, and I'm setting you free. Right now, right here." Jesus is giving you an opportunity to have a fresh start no matter what lies behind you. That is pretty amazing news! You are free to move forward with a light heart and soul.

Everyone has sinned and
is far away from God's saving presence.
But by the free gift of God's grace all are put right with Him
through Christ Jesus, who sets them free.
ROMANS 3:23-24 GNT

Because of His kindness,
you have been saved through trusting Christ.
And even trusting is not of yourselves;
it too is a gift from God.
EPHESIANS 2:8 TLB

We believe that we are all saved the same way,
by the undeserved grace of the Lord Jesus.

ACTS 15:11 NLT

Prayer

Jesus, thank You for setting me free with Your grace.
Thank You for the Gospel.

The Messy And The Mundane

Dreaming big for the Lord means one wild adventure. It means you never know what's coming next because He's full of surprises. Dreaming big for the Lord means you live ready to live out God's plan and purpose for your life. But that doesn't mean that it's all going to be exciting. It's not all going to be sunshine and rainbows and sparkles falling from clouds in the sky. No, some days are going to be really messy and some days are going to be really mundane. Some days you're going to be living your best life and other days you're going to be folding laundry and doing dishes. But remember this: Sometimes God grows us the most in the messy and mundane. Sometimes those days are the days He uses the small things to teach us big lessons. The best thing we can do is to learn how to find joy in every single season we're in. The exciting, crazy, wild days and the messy ones when we're just trying to survive. There is purpose in all of our days, so let's find joy in them.

The Lord is close to all who call on Him,
yes, to all who call on Him in truth.
PSALM 145:18 NLT

When I look at your heavens, the work of your fingers,
the moon and the stars, which you have set in place,
what is man that you are mindful of him,
and the son of man that you care for him?
PSALM 8:3-4 ESV

And the Lord will guide you continually,
and satisfy you with all good things,
and keep you healthy too;
and you will be like a well-watered garden,
like an ever-flowing spring.

ISAIAH 58:11 TLB

Prayer

Lord, find me in the messy and the mundane.
Teach me how to find joy in every season.

Finding Joy In Grief

Grief is a tricky thing to have to explain. There are all sorts of stages, and just when you think you're over one, another one hits. You'll be fine one day and a mess the next. And while grief gets easier over time, it never really leaves you. It's always there, lingering.

If you've experienced a loss of any sort—whether it's a loved one, a relationship, a failed dream, something you've had to let go of—you will have really, really strong days. When you feel like you've conquered the pain and you're able to move on. And then you wake up the next morning and you feel everything all over again. And then some days, you're in between stages, and all you're wanting is to be on the other side. Don't lose hope in these moments. Find joy in them. This is when God is working in you. And hold onto hope. You *are* going to come out on the other side. And so much stronger than before.

What's the price of a pet canary? Some loose change, right?
And God cares what happens to it even more than you do.
He pays even greater attention to you, down to the last detail—
even numbering the hairs on your head!
MATTHEW 10:29-30 THE MESSAGE

The Lord lifts the fallen and
those bent beneath their loads.
PSALM 145:14 TLB

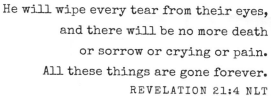
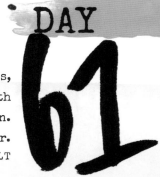

He will wipe every tear from their eyes,
and there will be no more death
or sorrow or crying or pain.
All these things are gone forever.
REVELATION 21:4 NLT

pRayer

God, on the days when it really hurts,
I know You're going to sustain me
through this grief.
Thank You for being faithful.

White Space

Graphic designers use a technique called "white space." White space is just a blank space around a page that is used in magazines, websites, logos, and other design elements to draw your eye to the main purpose for the design. It is actually not always white at all, it's just blank. It allows your eyes to "breathe" so that when they focus on the main element of the page, they find harmony and balance within the design. White space is what designers use to remind the viewer that a page *full* of text and pictures is not necessary to create a clear and beautiful message.

The same can be said of us and how God uses quieter seasons in our lives. Life doesn't always have to feel chaotic and full. Sometimes the most still and silent days are the ones that draw our eyes to the things that matter most. The quiet can make us appreciate the loud in our day to day. It gives us room to breathe in the midst of chaos so we can focus on the most important things in our lives. So don't lose hope when you're in a slower, quieter season. God is working on you even in the quiet, "white" space.

Listen, O Job, stop and consider the wonderful miracles of God.
JOB 37:14 TLB

He lets me lie down in green pastures;
He leads me beside quiet waters.
PSALM 23:2 HCSB

Be still in the presence of the LORD,
and wait patiently for Him to act.

PSALM 37:7 NLT

Prayer

Lord, in the quiet, white space,
show me the things that matter most.

Never Lose Sight

The state flower of California is the poppy. They're vibrant orange and beautiful. And every few years, after a winter with plenty of rain, there's a mountainside in the southern part of the state that has huge blooms filling over seventeen hundred acres with beautiful orange poppies. It is such a rare occurrence that it creates quite the frenzy, causing standstill traffic on the freeways and clogging up the pathways. It's rare, exquisitely beautiful, and dreamy. Everyone wants to catch a glimpse.

But what if the poppies were always there, readily available for anyone to just take a look? Would people appreciate them as much? Would they still cause traffic jams and all-out mania? Probably not.

It's easy to lose sight of the amazingness of God when we have access to Him 24/7. Seriously think about it: we have a direct line to the Creator of the universe and He loves us, He thinks we're beautiful, and He wants us to have a meaningful relationship with Him. Wow. We should stand in awe and wonder of this beautiful, breathtaking fact every day, every hour, every minute of our lives.

You alone are the LORD. You made the heavens,
even the highest heavens, and all their starry host,
the earth and all that is on it, the seas and all that is in them.
You give life to everything,
and the multitudes of heaven worship You.
NEHEMIAH 9:6 NIV

I will never fail you.
I will never abandon you.
HEBREWS 13:5 NLT

prayer

Lord, remind me daily of Your awesome beauty
so I will never lose sight of how truly amazing You are.

God Sees A Beautiful Future

Zacchaeus was a sneaky little tax collector. Jesus found him in a tree. Once Zacchaeus met Jesus, he turned his life around, made things right with people, and gave away half of his money. God found Joseph in prison. He was in prison because he had been falsely accused of something. Once he was found by God, he was able to forgive his accusers and do great things for the Lord. God found a teenage David herding sheep in a field. He called him to be king, and David went on to change the world for God. Jesus found Paul while Paul was persecuting and killing people who believed in Him. When Paul was found by Jesus, he changed his life around and became one of the loudest voices for the Gospel in the Bible.

If you think your life is not worthy enough to be used, let these examples change your perspective. God oftentimes finds us when we're at our worst, not our best. When people see failure in us, God sees a beautiful future. He will use you and your story to further His kingdom if you are willing to let Him.

> "Zacchaeus!" he said. "Quick! Come down!
> For I am going to be a guest in your home today!"
> LUKE 19:5 TLB

> The warden had no more worries,
> because Joseph took care of everything.
> The LORD was with him and caused everything he did to succeed.
> GENESIS 39:23 NLT

But God had mercy on me so that Christ Jesus
could use me as an example to show everyone
how patient He is with even the worst sinners,
so that others will realize that they, too,
can have everlasting life.

I TIMOTHY 1:16 TLB

PRayer

Thank You for finding me at my worst, Jesus.
Now I want to give You my best. Use me here.

Perfect Plan

Sometimes our plans and our paths fit perfectly into a box and can be tied with a bow. A perfect pregnancy. Escrow closing perfectly on a new house. Getting accepted into your first college choice. But sometimes things don't work out. They don't fit a plan and they don't bring closure. And you're left wondering what happened and how to move forward. There is still hope here. You can still be assured that God's peace is still there, surpassing your understanding. You can be assured that God knows and understands how you feel and that even though there may be confusion, He is not leaving you alone. Let His Word carry you through the uncertainty and find the freedom to move on from the broken plan and anticipate with joy what He has perfectly planned for your future.

You will keep in perfect peace
all who trust in You,
all whose thoughts are fixed on You!
ISAIAH 26:3 NLT

So do not fear, for I am with you;
do not be dismayed, for I am your God.
I will strengthen you and help you;
I will uphold you with My righteous right hand.
ISAIAH 41:10 NIV

Now may the Lord of peace Himself give you peace
at all times and in every way.
The Lord be with all of you.
II THESSALONIANS 3:16 NIV

DAY
65

For God gave us a spirit not of fear
but of power and love and self-control.
II TIMOTHY 1:7 ESV

Prayer

Lord, I don't understand what's happening right now
but I know You've got it all under control.
Thank You for not leaving me alone.

God's Pace

It can be hard to continually have to say, "I'm so happy for you," when good things are happening to people around you and you're wondering when it will be your turn. It can be even harder to actually feel that happiness in your heart when you're focused on the things you're waiting on. Bitterness and jealousy can creep in and take over, and it's almost like you have to say those happy words from behind clenched teeth.

Take heart and have hope. It feels far away right now, but God is working in this space. He's teaching you to be strong and to not give up. Because when you finally arrive at the place God is leading you to, you'll be so glad you went at His pace and waited on His timing. So as you watch others around you experience things you're waiting on, find God's grace there. Allow it to wash over you in the waiting.

Love is patient, love is kind.
Love does not envy,
is not boastful, is not conceited.
I CORINTHIANS 13:4 HCSB

A peaceful heart leads to a healthy body;
jealousy is like cancer in the bones.
PROVERBS 14:30 NLT

A sweet friendship refreshes the soul.
PROVERBS 27:9 THE MESSAGE

prayer

Lord, help me find joy in the happiness of others around me,
even when I don't feel like it. I pray against all bitterness
and jealousy and hand it over to You.

Telling Your Story

Do you have a favorite book? There is something about that story that makes it your favorite. Maybe it's the characters. Maybe it's the mystery. Maybe it's the ending. Maybe it's the way the book makes you feel. Whatever it is, chances are that you've told at least one person to read the book and why you loved it as much as you do.

Everyone has their own story. Some of our stories are action-packed and full. Some are quieter and calmer. But we all have one. Our stories tell of the journey God has taken us on and the things He's done in our lives. And every story has characters, plots, conflicts, and resolutions, just like your favorite book. We have a choice. We can either keep our story to ourselves or we can share it with others and bring God glory through the process. Why not tell the world what He's done for us?

Thank GOD! Call out His Name!
Tell the whole world who He is
and what He's done!
I CHRONICLES 16:8 THE MESSAGE

Therefore, go and make disciples
of all the nations.
MATTHEW 28:19 NLT

DAY
67

But have reverence
for Christ in your hearts,
and honor Him as Lord.
Be ready at all times
to answer anyone who asks you
to explain the hope you have.
I PETER 3:15 GNT

Jesus! Thank You for saving me.
Thank You for giving me the story You've given me.
Help me use it for Your glory every chance I get.

Your Worth In Jesus

Have you ever heard of the story of the woman who poured perfume on Jesus' feet? Jesus was visiting a friend for dinner, and when this woman, a prostitute, heard that Jesus was in the village, she took her most expensive bottle of perfume over to the house. When she stood in the presence of Jesus, she was overcome with emotion as she wept. She bent down and took her perfume and poured it on Jesus' feet. The friend of Jesus was shocked, asking Jesus, "Don't you know what kind of woman You're allowing to touch you?" But Jesus said to His friend, "Her sins are forgiven! Her faith has saved her. She is able to go in peace." Jesus forgave her, comforted her, and defended her.

Do not let anyone make you question your worth in Jesus. No matter what you've done and where you've come from, Jesus has called you His own. He has called you worthy, He has called you forgiven. He goes before you, He comforts you, and He defends you. And then He calls you to go in peace. That is pretty amazing!

But God put His love on the line for us by offering His Son
in sacrificial death while we were of no use whatever to Him.
ROMANS 5:8 THE MESSAGE

I give them eternal life,
and they will never perish—ever!
No one will snatch them out of My hand.
JOHN 10:28 HCSB

The name of the LORD is a strong tower;
the righteous man runs into it and is safe.

PROVERBS 18:10 ESV

Prayer

Thank You, Jesus,
for calling me worthy, forgiven, and Yours.
Let Your peace wash over me today.

Live It Up

We all say these kinds of things: "I don't have time for this!" or "I wish I had more time today!" or "This could not come at a worse time!" It seems like at one point or another, we all wish we could just magically slip a few extra hours into the day so that we could get more done, check more off our to-do lists, and not feel so rushed. However, as hard as we try, we can't give our lives more time. It just doesn't work that way. We have twenty-four hours a day for the rest of our lives. So why not change our perspective? Instead of wishing we could give our lives more time, why not give our time more life? Why not live it harder, better, more glorifying to the Lord? Why not dream bigger, pray stronger, and seek out our passions to the fullest?

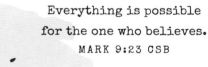

For God gave us a spirit not of fear
but of power and love and self-control.
II TIMOTHY 1:7 ESV

Everything is possible
for the one who believes.
MARK 9:23 CSB

I can do all things through him
who strengthens me.

PHILIPPIANS 4:13 ESV

DAY 69

prayer

Lord, wake me from my sleep
and open my eyes to the huge dreams
You have for me. Give me the strength, wisdom,
and passion to pursue them with all my heart.

Hearing God's Voice

Wouldn't it be amazing if we could actually converse with God? To be able to ask Him questions and audibly *hear* His reply? And to be able to ask Him what the plan is and not have to wait for an answer? It would make conversations with Him not seem so one-sided. It would be so easy to just be able to say, "Hey, God, here is my deepest desire. Can we talk about how to make that happen and when?"

That's not how it works with God, though. And oftentimes, I think we ask Him to speak to us and we wait for this loud, audible voice that cannot be mistaken for anyone other than God. We keep waiting for that, and in that waiting, we miss countless ways He actually is speaking. We miss the ways He's whispering directly to our hearts—in a sunset, in a worship song, in a kind deed from a stranger. When we are constantly searching for God in the loud ways, we miss hearing Him in all the quiet ways. How can you hear God in the quiet ways today?

Call to me and I will answer you,
and will tell you great and hidden things
that you have not known.
JEREMIAH 33:3 ESV

And if you leave God's paths and go astray,
you will hear a voice behind you say,
"No, this is the way; walk here."
ISAIAH 30:21 TLB

My sheep recognize My voice.
I know them, and they follow Me.
JOHN 10:27 THE MESSAGE

PRayer

Lord, help me be quiet enough
to hear You speak to me in the loud ways and the quiet ways.
Help me know Your voice above all else.

WORSHIP WITH ALL YOUR HEART

When God calls us to a time of worship, He wants us in our most real state of mind. He doesn't want perfectly pitched voices singing the words with hands raised high in the air. He wants our hearts—surrendered to Him in honest worship. He simply wants our hallelujahs—when they're rejoicing and when they're confused. When they're excited and when they're tired. He wants us to worship when we're happy and worship when we're hurting. He wants our worshipping hearts when they feel full and when they feel broken. When we bring our honest, surrendered hearts to a place of worship, we see His faithfulness, even when we don't understand it. We find His grace in that surrendered place as He begins to reveal Himself to us.

Humble yourselves before the Lord,
and He will lift you up in honor.
JAMES 4:10 NLT

He is your praise and He is your God,
who has done for you these great and awe-inspiring works
your eyes have seen.
DEUTERONOMY 10:21 CSB

DAY

71

We praise You, God,
we praise You, for Your Name is near;
people tell of Your wonderful deeds.

PSALM 75:1 NIV

Prayer

Jesus, I surrender all of me to You.
Take my heart, my soul, my body and fill me with Your presence.
I will worship You all of my days.

Falling In Love With Jesus

One definition of the word *dream* is "indulging in daydreams about something greatly desired." When we step back and think about what we greatly desire in our lives, so many things can come to mind. Dream job, traveling, marriage, beautiful home, a healthy family, close relationships—the list can go on and on. All of those things are wonderful; they're things that we all greatly desire from time to time. But what if we shift our focus? What if we switch up our dreams? When we switch our thinking from dreaming about our future to dreaming about falling more and more passionately in love with Jesus, we allow ourselves to be surrendered to His plan and our hearts become more aligned with His throughout the journey we are on with Him. The more we pursue God and spend time with Him, the more we fall in love with who God is, His character, and who He is continually creating us to be. Falling more and more in love with God is such a beautiful thing. Let it lead your heart today.

God is love,
and anyone who lives in love is living with God
and God is living in him.
I JOHN 4:16 TLB

How precious is Your unfailing love, O God!
PSALM 36:7 NLT

Trust steadily in God,
hope unswervingly, love extravagantly.
And the best of the three is love.
I CORINTHIANS 13:13 THE MESSAGE

PRAYER

Jesus, my greatest desire is
to love You with all my heart, soul, and mind.
Today, I will choose to pursue You above anything else.

Pursuing Your Passions

If you're passionate about cooking, then you know that you can never stop becoming a better chef. You can spend countless hours learning new things—all about spices, all about sauces, all about different techniques you can use. You can read books and recipes, and then you can put everything you are learning into practice. You can create a masterpiece with your food—blending colors and spices and smells and flavors all into one beautiful dish. And when it's all said and done, you can keep learning and growing in your knowledge of cooking, and you can keep trying new things.

It's the same with Jesus. When we're passionate about loving Him and following Him, we never want to stop learning about Him. We crave reading His Word and we look forward to spending time with Him. We constantly figure out new ways to love Him better, like praying, journaling, worshipping. And we spend time learning His attributes and who He really is as our Savior. This is the best possible passion to have. And the more we follow hard after Him, the sweeter it gets and the more we desire His heart.

Seek the Lord; yes, seek His strength and seek His face untiringly.
I CHRONICLES 16:11 TLB

It is impossible to please God without faith.
Anyone who wants to come to Him must believe that God exists
and that He rewards those who sincerely seek Him.
HEBREWS 11:6 NLT

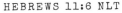

153

You will seek Me,
and you will find Me because
you will seek Me with all your heart.
JEREMIAH 29:13 GNT

prayer

Lord, I never want to stop
learning about You. Teach me Your ways!
I long to be more passionate about You.

Yes

Have you ever had a season of life where it just feels like every door is being closed on you? Not just closed but *slammed*. It feels like every single answer you're waiting on and praying for is no. You know the way hot, frustrated tears feel when they spill onto your cheeks? It feels like *that* over and over again. You've been waiting and hopeful, and you're not even sure how to move forward anymore. You're disappointed and maybe even angry that God is saying no to all your plans.

Maybe He is using this season to shape you. He's using all these *no's* to make you fix your eyes directly on things above—directly on Him. God's using this time to remind you that He loves you and that He has a perfect plan for your life, no matter how it might seem right now. He's using this time to teach you to keep your eyes on eternity and all that is going to come. And pretty soon, before you know it, you are going to finally hear a YES. God is a faithful God who does not go back on His promises.

I have complete confidence, O God;
I will sing and praise You!
PSALM 57:7 GNT

Let your eyes look directly forward,
and your gaze be straight before you.
PROVERBS 4:25 ESV

Oh, that my steps might be steady,
keeping to the course You set.
PSALM 119:6 THE MESSAGE

Prayer

Lord, I pray that in all of these no's,
I'll continue to trust in Your YES.
Thank You for not going back on Your promises.

A Long Desert

Did you know that California was in a very serious drought for seven years? The rain was so sparse that everywhere you looked, all you saw was brown. People put "Pray For Rain" bumper stickers on their cars, and most of the state was on water regulations. Lawns could only be watered on certain days, and showers could only be a certain number of minutes. It felt like a very long desert, and it felt like no rain was going to cure this.

It can sometimes feel like we are in the same long desert. Where life feels dry and stagnant and we're not sure when rain is going to come. Have hope. One day soon, the floodgates are going to open, and God is going to rain down His mercy on you so hard that you'll be swept up quickly into His arms. Hold onto that hope. He does not leave us and He does not let us down.

For I will pour water on the thirsty ground
and send streams coursing through the parched earth.
ISAIAH 44:3 THE MESSAGE

O God, you are my God;
earnestly I seek you;
my soul thirsts for you;
my flesh faints for you,
as in a dry and weary land
where there is no water.
PSALM 63:1 ESV

He changed deserts into pools of water
and dry land into flowing springs.

PSALM 107:35 GNT

PRAYER

Thank You for Your mercies, Jesus.
Thank You for never leaving me
and never letting me down.

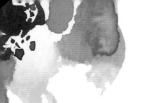

Rising Up

If you've ever baked a cake, then you know that it can take a good forty-five minutes to cook completely. And the delicious aroma the cake produces as it gets closer to being finished makes it hard to keep that oven door closed nice and tight until the beep goes off announcing it's complete. But it's extremely important to keep the oven door closed until the cake is finished baking because when you allow cooler air into the oven, it prevents your cake from rising beautifully.

It's easy to do the same thing as we wait on the Lord. We get impatient and we want to take the timing into our own hands. But God's plan and recipe for our lives is so much better than our own! He is cooking up something wonderful for our lives, and the best thing we can do is to not rush Him or His timing. And when it is all said and done, we will rise up beautifully, for His glory and not our own.

The Lord is wonderfully good
to those who wait for Him,
to those who seek for Him.
LAMENTATIONS 3:25 TLB

We also pray that you will be strengthened
with all His glorious power
so you will have all the endurance and patience you need.
COLOSSIANS 1:11 NLT

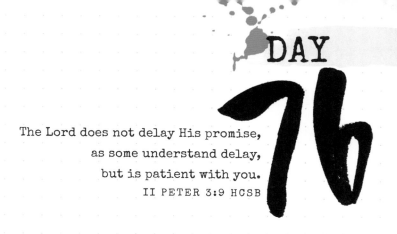

DAY 76

The Lord does not delay His promise,
as some understand delay,
but is patient with you.

II PETER 3:9 HCSB

PRAYER

I will wait on Your timing today, God.
I know it may not look like mine,
but I trust in You for Your perfect plans!

Your Purpose

When God created you, He created you with a purpose and a calling for your life. He created you to have talents and desires and strengths and weaknesses. He created you with things that will come easy for you and also attributes that you will have to work very hard at. He created you with dreams and aspirations, things you will run hard after, passions you will pursue with your entire heart.

The more we pursue God, the more we discover what that purpose and calling is. The more we seek His heart and seek His face, the more we learn about who God desires us to be. The more we turn to Him for every area of our lives, the more we learn that *He* is what we will begin to desire to run hard after, *He* will become the greatest passion we pursue with our entire heart.

But collect for yourselves treasures in heaven,
where neither moth nor rust destroys,
and where thieves don't break in and steal.
MATTHEW 6:20 HCSB

Now seek the LORD your God with all your heart and soul.
I CHRONICLES 22:19 NLT

DAY

77

I love all who love me.
Those who search for me
shall surely find me.
PROVERBS 8:17 TLB

Prayer

Thank You for creating me with a purpose, God.
I want to run hard after You and Your will for my life.

Being A Light

Ruth married into a family and shortly after lost her husband, her brother-in-law, and her father-in-law....meaning her mother-in-law, Naomi, lost her husband and two sons all on the same day. Ruth had every right to flee the situation and start over. She could have left to grieve in her own timing and in her own way. But she chose to stay—not because she wanted a pat on the back, but because Ruth refused to let her mother-in-law grieve alone. Ruth didn't hesitate when it came to showing loyalty, unconditional love, and self-sacrifice to Naomi, a friend who was hurting and was in need. Do you know someone enduring extreme loss? It's easy to say a quick, *praying for you*, as you pass by them in grocery store, or drop a quick note in the mail—but the hard work comes when you're willing to sit with them in their pain, walk with them through the valley, and be a constant reminder of the light at the end of the tunnel. Ask God to fill your mouth with the right words, your hands with the actions, and your heart with the right motives. He will show you the way.

But Ruth replied, "Don't urge me to leave you or to turn back from you.
Where you go I will go, and where you stay I will stay.
Your people will be my people and your God my God."
RUTH 1:16 NIV

Carry one another's burdens;
in this way you will fulfill the law of Christ.
GALATIANS 6:2 CSB

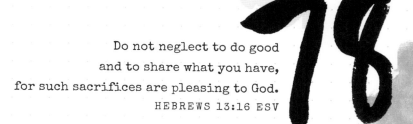

Do not neglect to do good
and to share what you have,
for such sacrifices are pleasing to God.
HEBREWS 13:16 ESV

prayer

Jesus, show me how to share Your love
the best way I can with those around me.
Open my eyes to those in pain,
and help me to react with the same loyalty,
unconditional love, and self-sacrifice as Ruth.

Pursuing God's Peace

Is there something causing you anxiety today? Something that is making you stressed or worried? Think about peace for a second. It is easy to talk about how God is our peace, but take a few minutes to *really think* about that and let it sink in. Just as much as we pursue our passions and our dreams, we need to pursue God's peace. Pursue God's peace that is far deeper than we can ever understand. When we allow God's peace to wash over us, it brings freedom from the battles in our minds. It frees us from the things that cause us anxiety—like mistakes, hurt feelings, bumps in our day. God's peace frees us from disappointments and heartache. It sets our hearts at *ease* despite our circumstances. Whatever you're walking through today, pursue His peace far more than you pursue your passions. He will keep His promises, and His peace will be far greater than you can understand.

And the peace of God,
which surpasses all understanding,
will guard your hearts
and your minds in Christ Jesus.
PHILIPPIANS 4:7 ESV

The LORD gives strength to His people
and blesses them with peace.
PSALM 29:11 GNT

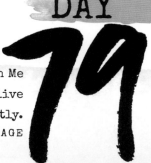

Keep company with Me
and you'll learn to live
freely and lightly.
MATTHEW 11:30 THE MESSAGE

Prayer

Forgive me, Jesus, for letting
my anxiety get the best of me today.
I hand my worries over to You today, Lord.
Let Your peace rule my heart.

Strong and Courageous

God's Word tells us over and over to be strong and courageous. Joshua 1:9 (THE MESSAGE) says, "Haven't I commanded you? Strength! Courage! Don't be timid; don't get discouraged. GOD, your God, is with you every step you take." As you're dreaming big for your future, there will be a lot of moments when you may feel afraid of what's next or anxious about answers you're waiting on. You may feel intimidated to make decisions or overwhelmed at possibilities before you, but listen to God's Word and *have courage*. A lot of "going for it" is allowing yourself to be bold and strong in your heart and your mind and reminding yourself as best as possible that God isn't leaving your side! He is with you every step you take as you embark on every adventure! He delights in it, actually. So as you set out today, remember the promises in His Word and be courageous.

So be strong and courageous! Do not be afraid and do not panic before them. For the LORD your God will personally go ahead of you. He will neither fail you nor abandon you.
DEUTERONOMY 31:6 NLT

Then he continued, "Be strong and courageous and get to work. Don't be frightened by the size of the task, for the Lord my God is with you; he will not forsake you. He will see to it that everything is finished correctly.
I CHRONICLES 28:20 TLB

Remember that I have commanded you
to be determined and confident!
Do not be afraid or discouraged, for I,
the LORD your God, am with you wherever you go.
JOSHUA 1:9 GNT

Prayer

Jesus, help me be bold and have courage as
I set out to follow my passions.
Calm my fears and give me the strength
to make big moves for You.

Where Life Starts

Our hearts have the capacity to feel emotions deeply all around the spectrum. To love deeply, to hurt deeply, to dream deeply. We oftentimes make decisions because of what our hearts feel, and when our hearts are involved, we are *all in*. And everything we do is dictated from this tender place, where the heart fuels our decisions, the things we value, the things we're willing to fight for. Your heart is where life starts. And because of that, the Bible tells you to guard it, to keep watch over it. When you are able to do this—to guard your heart, to watch your steps— the path God is leading you on will stretch out before you. Because your heart is where life starts, God has created it with such depth— with purpose and intention—and when we guard it and protect it, we allow only the things in that God intended for us. And the outcome is a passion that can change the world around us. Our hearts are fragile and tender but powerful and can be used to bring glory to God in the very best way. How can you guard your heart more carefully today?

Guard your heart above all else,
for it determines the course of your life.
PROVERBS 4:23 NLT

Prove me, O LORD, and try me;
test my heart and my mind.
PSALM 26:2 ESV

DAY 81

Happy are those whose hearts are pure,
for they shall see God.

MATTHEW 5:8 TLB

prayer

You have created my inmost being, Lord.
You know my heart better than anyone else.
Help me guard it, Jesus, so that I can bring You glory.

When We get Knocked Down

Winston Churchill once said, "Courage is going from failure to failure without losing enthusiasm." The thing about dreaming big for the Lord and with the Lord is that there is not always a perfect outcome. We will have disappointments, we will make mistakes. We will have heartache and we will fail sometimes. But God is on our side. And He never leaves it. He gives us courage to keep going, to keep picking ourselves back up when we get knocked down. And He gives us strength to keep finding joy and enthusiasm in our circumstances—even when things don't feel very joyful. So when things feel like they're falling apart and you're not sure how you're going to pick yourself back up, be reminded that God is giving you the courage to keep going. And to keep going with the joy of the Lord on your side.

We can rejoice, too, when we run into problems and trials,
for we know that they are good for us—
they help us learn to be patient.
ROMANS 5:3 TLB

Even though the fig trees are all destroyed,
and there is neither blossom left nor fruit;
though the olive crops all fail, and the fields lie barren;
even if the flocks die in the fields and the cattle barns are empty,
yet I will rejoice in the Lord; I will be happy in the God
of my salvation.
HABAKKUK 3:17–18 TLB

Weeping may last through the night,
but joy comes with the morning.
PSALM 30:5 NLT

Prayer

Lord, I know that disappointments
and failures build character.
Help me get back up again when I feel like
everything is falling apart.

Let God Win

If you're feeling any heaviness or anxiety at this very moment, stop and take a deep breath. And when you do, allow yourself to make a decision. No matter how hard this day becomes, no matter how overwhelmed you feel, no matter how lonely you become, do not let those things win over you. Let God win. Life is not perfect, nor is today. But God is. And so is His grace and His mercy. And He will guide you through the heaviness of today and take you exactly where you need to be. And because of that, there is no reason to fear the future or to feel overwhelmed by it. You will have everything you need. So for today, take a deep breath. Let His overwhelming grace wash over your overwhelming anxiety and in that, find the joy and strength you need to make it through this day.

Don't fret or worry.
Instead of worrying, pray.
Let petitions and praises
shape your worries into prayers,
letting God know your concerns.
PHILIPPIANS 4:6 THE MESSAGE

Such love has no fear,
because perfect love expels all fear.
I JOHN 4:18 NLT

Anxiety in a man's heart weighs him down,
but a good word makes him glad.
PROVERBS 12:25 ESV

Prayer

God, You are perfect and so are Your ways.
When I feel overwhelmed, give me peace
that calms my anxious heart.

grace Upon grace

Sometimes, when we're in seasons of expectation and waiting, it can be hard to see the things God has placed right in front of us—especially when others have what we're longing for. In moments of discontentment, it can be hard to focus on things that bring us joy. But just pause for a moment, and take a big look at your life. See all the beauty that God has placed right in front of you. Look around you and see the little pockets of grace that He has graciously arranged in different corners of your life. They're little reminders to keep trusting in Him, to keep believing that He has the sweetest plan for your life. He's reminding you to continue being patient in this place, to keep persevering and to not give up. He's whispering, *There is still beauty in the waiting, and one day you're going to realize it was all worth it.* The waiting will one day make sense. When you look around you and see the beauty and see God's little grace notes, you will be able to find sweet contentment in Him alone.

For from his fullness we have all received,

grace upon grace.

JOHN 1:16 ESV

But whatever I am now it is all

because God poured out such kindness and grace upon me.

I CORINTHIANS 15:10 TLB

DAY

84

But grace was given to each one of us
according to the measure of Christ's gift.

EPHESIANS 4:7 ESV

PRayer

God, show me Your grace today
through little pockets of beauty around me.
Remind me of the gifts You have given me
in times where I forget.

Thirsting

We all go through periods of time in our lives where following hard after the Lord and believing what His Word says comes a little bit more difficult for us. It feels like a desert—a dry land, where we're thirsting for God's love, His plan, His certainty, and we're coming up dry. It's good for us to go through wildernesses like this, where we have to pursue Him and push into Him, even when we don't feel like it. But it's in this wilderness that God is chasing after you so much harder than you could ever imagine. His goodness is running after you. In those moments of uncertainty, when you're just not sure if His way is what you want to follow anymore, His love is what will lead you back. And there is where you will find His open arms, waiting for you, full of redemption, acceptance, and grace. It'll be like a tall glass of water.

Teach me to see what I still don't see.
JOB 34:32 THE MESSAGE

Immediately the father of the child cried out and said,
"I believe; help my unbelief!"
MARK 9:24 ESV

What's more, I am with you,
and will protect you wherever you go,
and will bring you back safely to this land;
I will be with you constantly
until I have finished giving you
all I am promising.

GENESIS 28:15 TLB

prayer

Lord, thank You for running after me.
Stay with me, Jesus, through all of my days.
I love You.

Getting To Dream Big

Have you ever counted how many times you say "I have to..." a day? From mundane things like "I have to go to work" and "I have to do the dishes" to spiritual things like "I have to pray about it" and even as far as "I'm having to wait on His timing." The result could be very daunting and overwhelming and leave you feeling rather frustrated. But what if you shifted your focus? What if you started to say things like, "I *get* to wait on God's timing" or "I *get* to dream big for the Lord and see what happens." While it may feel hard and unnatural, it will begin to transform your thinking. We oftentimes look at things that feel overwhelming in a negative way, and that causes us to feel stressed or anxious when thinking about them. But if we begin to think optimistically about things instead, they become blessings in our lives instead of stresses. What are some ways you can change your thinking from "have to" to "get to" today?

Fill your minds with those things
that are good and that deserve praise:
things that are true, noble, right, pure, lovely, and honorable.
PHILIPPIANS 4:8 GNT

Never tire of loyalty and kindness.
Hold these virtues tightly.
Write them deep within your heart.
PROVERBS 3:3 TLB

A cheerful heart is good medicine,
but a broken spirit saps a person's strength.
PROVERBS 17:22 NLT

Prayer

Lord, I GET to live my life for You today
and follow after my dreams!
Thank You for the opportunity to live for You.

The Way There

If you've ever gone on a backpacking trip, then you know how much goes into the planning part of it. You plan the course, you map routes, you prepare for the journey. You set your sights on the destination and everything you need to do to get there. You hit the final stretch and you anticipate the end of the journey. And when you finally get there, no matter how long the route is, you are proud of yourself for making it as far as you did.

But anyone who has backpacked knows it's not always about the end. It's also about the way there. The now. It's about the scenery on the path, the mistakes you make on the way. It's about figuring out the solution to unexpected problems that come up. It's about pushing yourself no matter how hard that trip gets, pushing yourself through the hard places and rough paths. It's about finishing the course you've set your sights on, even when you're scared and even when it seems impossible. Because with God, *all* things are possible.

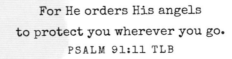

"Go in peace," the priest replied.
"For the Lord is watching over your journey."
JUDGES 18:6 NLT

For He orders His angels
to protect you wherever you go.
PSALM 91:11 TLB

DAY 87

We plan the way we want to live,
but only GOD makes us able to live it.
PROVERBS 16:9 THE MESSAGE

prayer

Jesus, with You all things are possible.
Help me find You during the journey,
not just at the destination.

He Is Holding You Close

Do you ever get into bed at the end of the day and think about everything that happened? The failures of the day are usually what captivate our minds as we wrestle with what we could have done differently if we had the chance to do it over. And if it was a *really* hard day, it can be difficult not to lose sleep or lie awake dwelling on mistakes. Listen, God meets you in that place. He whispers in those moments, "You're forgiven and free from these failures." He knows your thoughts and He knows your heart and He's not leaving you in that place. The hardships can make us feel weighed down, but God is gently saying, "I will carry that load for you." He is holding you close, grabbing hold of your heart, and freeing your mind from the burdens you're carrying. And then He is giving you a fresh new day when you wake up—with no mistakes yet. Find your hope here in Him.

You're my place of quiet retreat;
I wait for Your Word to renew me.
PSALM 119:114 THE MESSAGE

But since we belong to the day,
we must be serious and put the armor
of faith and love on our chests,
and put on a helmet of the hope of salvation.
I THESSALONIANS 5:8 HCSB

DAY 88

He will wipe every tear from their eyes,
and there will be no more death
or sorrow or crying or pain.
All these things are gone forever.
REVELATION 21:4 NLT

PRAYER

Lord, please free me
from feelings of guilt and shame.
Help me to release any thoughts
that don't come directly from You.
I want to live in Your hope.

Worth It

There will be a day coming soon when you will wake up and you will realize that it was all worth it. Whatever journey God has taken you on as you've dreamed your heart out, whatever paths He's made you walk down—it was all part of His plan. And you're going to be thankful. You're going to be thankful for the times God changed your direction and took you a different route. You're going to understand God's heart better. His desires for your life will become clearer. And you're going to realize that God may not have given you what you wanted, but He gave you what He knows you needed. And you're going to be so grateful that you trusted Him with your dreams. He truly knows every intricate place in our hearts, and He is so *good* to us even when we don't understand His plan until the very end.

You can be sure that God
will take care of everything you need,
His generosity exceeding even yours in the glory
that pours from Jesus.
PHILIPPIANS 4:19 THE MESSAGE

For our present troubles are small and won't last very long.
Yet they produce for us a glory that vastly outweighs them and will
last forever! So we don't look at the troubles we can see now;
rather, we fix our gaze on things that cannot be seen.
II CORINTHIANS 4:17-18 NLT

DAY
89

Yet what we suffer now
is nothing compared to
the glory He will give us later.

ROMANS 8:18 TLB

Prayer

God, I trust You with my dreams.
I am thankful for the path You're guiding me on,
no matter where it leads me.

Pop-Ups

Have you ever been to a website that has a pesky pop-up ad? Every time you click something on the page, the pop-up ad is right there to remind you to join their email list for 10 percent off your next order. It can be rather annoying, to the point where you finally unwillingly join so that you don't have to see the pop-up anymore.

There are oftentimes the same kind of pop-ups in our own lives. Things that we are reminded of that we like to ignore so that we don't have to deal with them anymore. Maybe it's a sin issue, maybe it's a decision we don't want to think about, maybe it's an area God wants us to work on. But God doesn't mind being pesky when He wants to get our attention. He will allow the "pop-up" so that we eventually give in and align our hearts with His. So think about giving in today, think about letting Him work on your heart. Chances are, you'll be really glad you did.

If they listen and obey Him,
then they will be blessed
with prosperity throughout their lives.
JOB 36:11 TLB

Anyone on God's side listens to God's words.
JOHN 8:47 THE MESSAGE

We keep looking to the LORD our God for His mercy,
just as servants keep their eyes on their master,
as a slave girl watches her mistress
for the slightest signal.

PSALM 123:2 NLT

PRAYER

God, show me the pop-ups today.
Reveal to me what it is that You're trying to tell me.
I put my trust and hope in You.

Exciting Expectations

When you're going for it—*really going for it*—there is going to be a lot of excitement about what God is doing in your life and what He has in store for you. And there will also be days when maybe you don't understand why His timing takes so long and it causes worry over the unknowns. Even in this place, live with excited expectation of what the Lord is doing. In those anxious moments when you don't quite understand God's timing, *serve* your heart out. Make the most of this period of life when things are unknown and use this time to serve the Lord with everything you are. You are going to get to the place God is taking you, so why not embrace this season and glorify the Lord in the process? Instead of feeling worried or anxious, ask yourself, *How can I serve the Lord today? How can I make the most of this day?*

So then, obey the commands that I have given you today;
love the Lord your God and serve Him with all your heart.
DEUTERONOMY 11:13 GNT

But be sure to fear the Lord and faithfully serve Him.
Think of all the wonderful things He has done for you.
I SAMUEL 12:24 NLT

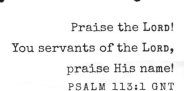

Praise the LORD!
You servants of the LORD,
praise His name!
PSALM 113:1 GNT

PRAYER

Instead of being focused on myself all the time,
Jesus, I'm going to work really hard
to serve You with my whole heart.
I want to bring You glory through the process!

God Is Carrying Us

Remember the saying, "Well don't just stand there, do something!" It's heard all the time in movies when there is a problem and no one quite knows how to fix it, so they just stand there panicking, staring at the issue instead of coming up with a solution.

Do you ever wonder if God feels like this about us? He sees the big picture and He sees our dreams and our deepest desires lying before us. He knows every thought and every worry and every hindrance. And sometimes I think God is saying, "Don't just stand there, do something with your life!" Fear and worry paralyze us and we panic instead of making the best out of a situation. We're insecure about the next steps to take, but we forget that we belong to a God who is carrying us in those moments.

The simple truth is that if you had a mere kernel of faith,
a poppy seed, say, you would tell this mountain,
"Move!" and it would move.
There is nothing you wouldn't be able to tackle.
MATTHEW 17:20 THE MESSAGE

Don't be afraid.
EXODUS 20:20 HCSB

My strength comes from GOD,
who made heaven, and earth,
and mountains.
PSALM 121:2 THE MESSAGE

Prayer

Jesus, You see the whole picture!
Remind me to put my faith
and trust in You when I start freezing under pressure.
You are in control of all things!

Childlike Imagination

A child's wild imagination is so fun to listen to. You can't help but smile at the way they think and the way they believe. Take their futures for example! When asked what they want to be when they grow up, most little kids say things like a football player, a princess, a fireman, or the president. And in their hearts, they believe it is all possible, not once doubting their strength or their ambitions.

We should be more like kids with our dreams. We should be able to believe the wildest things for our lives and lay them before the Lord with great hope. We should then be able to trust that He is going to do amazing things with those dreams! How can you have a childlike imagination today?

God has given each of us the ability
to do certain things well.
ROMANS 12:6 TLB

For we are his workmanship,
created in Christ Jesus for good works,
which God prepared beforehand,
that we should walk in them.
EPHESIANS 2:10 ESV

Jesus said,
"Let the children come to Me
and do not stop them,
because the Kingdom of heaven
belongs to such as these."

MATTHEW 19:14 GNT

DAY 93

PRAYER

I want to have faith like a child, Lord!
I want to live out a wild imagination for the Kingdom.
I believe You will do amazing things.

So Much More

Did you ever take ballet classes when you were a little girl and then dream of being a ballerina? Or maybe you took gymnastics as a kid and dreamed of going to the Olympics. Oftentimes as children, we believe in ourselves so much that we actually *think* we are capable of these things. And then as we get older, reality sets in, and we realize the potential for those dreams to happen probably isn't going to work out.

While we may not become ballerinas or Olympic gold medalists, the desire to be so much more was put there by God for a reason. *He* believes we are capable of doing more than we could ever believe possible—and He wants us to use those dreams and passions to point people back to Him. And we can't do any of that without Him. God created us with wild dreams so that He can teach us how much we need Him, to show us how to live our lives for Him, and to teach us how to glorify Him when He makes our dreams happen. So keep on dreaming those impossible dreams. You were created for this.

I am the vine; you are the branches.
Whoever abides in me and I in him,
he it is that bears much fruit,
for apart from me you can do nothing.
JOHN 15:5 ESV

But whatever is good and perfect comes to us from God,
the Creator of all light.
JAMES 1:17 TLB

DAY 94

He must become greater and greater,
and I must become less and less.

JOHN 3:30 NLT

PRayer

Jesus, You created me with
a passion and a purpose for a reason—
to live them out for You alone.
It's all about You, Jesus!
I can't do any of this on my own.

God Has The Final Say

As a mom, you have a lot of prayers, hopes, and dreams for your children. You pray they are kind to others and that they find the lonely kid in the lunch room. You pray they are smart and healthy. You pray they live life to their fullest and that they're strong and courageous. You pray that they end up doing something amazing with their lives. And most of all, you pray that they will fall in love with Jesus and choose to tell others all about Him.

But in reality, moms really only have so much say in what happens. They can dream their hearts out for their children, but ultimately, only God has the final say. You know the awesome part about that? God's dreams for His children are so much bigger and better than we could ever dare to imagine. So we trust in Him with our future, because we know it will turn out even better than we can ever hope for.

The LORD is my strength and my song;
He has given me victory.
EXODUS 15:2 NLT

And I am sure of this,
that he who began a good work in you will bring it
to completion at the day of Jesus Christ.
PHILIPPIANS 1:6 ESV

DAY 95

If you want to know what God wants you to do,
ask Him, and He will gladly tell you,
for He is always ready to give a bountiful supply
of wisdom to all who ask Him;
He will not resent it.

JAMES 1:5 TLB

Prayer

Lord, I lay all of the big plans I've dreamed up
at Your feet and surrender them all to You.
I know You have a much bigger and better dream for my life!

Sprouting Up

Have you ever been walking on a sidewalk somewhere and you look down to see a wildflower growing through a crack? It's always surprising because for all practical purposes, a wildflower isn't really supposed to grow through cement. But somehow it did.

Sometimes, against all odds, flowers will grow wherever they can find a small crack of sunlight or a glimmer of hope. The small crack in the sidewalk is what the flower needed to break free and ultimately spread just a little beauty to anyone who walked by. We might not always know where or how we need to sprout up, but as long as we're finding the Light, we will break free and keep growing. So even if you feel unsure of the future or the next steps, keep turning your eyes to Jesus and stay focused on His plan, and He will grow you and take you exactly where you need to go.

Therefore, as you received Christ Jesus the Lord,
so walk in him, rooted and built up in him
and established in the faith, just as you were taught,
abounding in thanksgiving.
COLOSSIANS 2:6–7 ESV

You will seek me and find me,
when you seek me with all your heart.
JEREMIAH 29:13 ESV

DAY
96

Let your eyes look forward;
fix your gaze straight ahead.
Carefully consider the path for your feet,
and all your ways will be established.
PROVERBS 4:25-26 CSB

PRAYER

Lord, whatever circumstances come my way,
help me to seek Your light through it.
Give me strength, wisdom, and courage
to blossom wherever You plant me.

Beauty From Ashes

You're at the end of your rope and you've exhausted all your resources. You've waited, you've prayed, you've cried countless tears. You've run the race, you've fought the good fight, and you're spent. You've been patient, you've been impatient. You've been angry and you've found joy. And yet, at the end of the day, every single door has been shut and every single answer has been no. So what do you do now?

You hold onto hope. You hold onto that hope so tightly because when all is said and done, you trust in Jesus and you are confident in His plan, no matter how distant it is from yours and how different it is from what you dreamed up. *There is still something beautiful that can come from this.* He will still turn this into something amazing. So look back and find awe in the journey and look forward and find hope in your future.

To all who mourn in Israel
He will give: beauty for ashes;
joy instead of mourning;
praise instead of heaviness.
ISAIAH 61:3 TLB

When he prays to God,
he will be accepted.
And God will receive him with joy
and restore him to good standing.
JOB 33:26 NLT

May the God of green hope fill you up
with joy, fill you up with peace,
so that your believing lives,
filled with the life-giving energy of
the Holy Spirit, will brim over with hope!
ROMANS 15:13 THE MESSAGE

pRayer

God, You turn ashes into beauty.
You will turn my failed dreams
into something beautiful.
While I don't understand it right now,
I have hope!

Stay Humble

If you've ever started your own business, you know how much work goes into it. There are so many things going on behind the scenes and a lot of pressure for it to work out. You pour your blood, sweat, and tears into it, and it is so rewarding when things start happening, when success starts coming your way. Celebrate each little success and joy! Take pride in your hard work and how far you've come. But, *stay humble* while doing so. God is blessing your socks off! He gave you the gifts and abilities you're using to get yourself this far. He deserves all the glory and the credit. When we start to let pride get in the way, it grieves God's Spirit and it makes it more about us than Him. So when you accomplish something huge, you deserve to be excited! Be delighted but not prideful. Be thankful but not entitled. And thank the Lord every step of the way that He's blessing you with amazing accomplishments. He deserves all the glory.

Since God chose you to be the holy people He loves,
you must clothe yourselves with tenderhearted mercy,
kindness, humility, gentleness, and patience.
COLOSSIANS 3:12 NLT

Be humble and gentle. Be patient with each other,
making allowance for each other's faults because of your love.
EPHESIANS 4:2 TLB

But the grace that God gives is even stronger.
As the scripture says, "God resists the proud,
but gives grace to the humble."

JAMES 4:6 GNT

Prayer

God, You have done amazing things for me! Keep me humble, Lord.
You deserve all the glory for all You've given to me.

Laughter Is The Best Medicine

Have you ever watched a singing competition show? I love to see the people who belt out tunes in the shower and think they're going to win the whole thing. They confidently walk onto the stage and think they've got the golden ticket before they even start, and then they start singing and their voice makes your ears bleed. You know they're about to hear a "NO" and their response is always highly anticipating. Will they throw a fit? Or laugh it off?

Sometimes we are just like those singers. There are a lot of opportunities that come our way that we will fail at. We can't be good at everything! So in those moments, we have a choice. We can either get mad and throw a fit...or we can laugh and take joy in it. God has a sense of humor, and these moments grow us into stronger people. So when you fail and get a big NO, take a deep breath and laugh. It's the best medicine!

A time to weep, and a time to laugh;
a time to mourn, and a time to dance.
ECCLESIASTES 3:4 ESV

He will yet fill your mouth with laughter
and your lips with a shout of joy.
JOB 8:21 HCSB

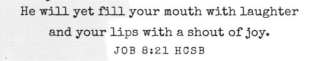

DAY 99

A cheerful heart is good medicine.

PROVERBS 17:22 NLT

PRAYER

I want to be someone who laughs with You
when things don't work the way I wanted them to.
Help me find joy in the failures, Lord!

Hoping Your Heart Out

In this book, you've read all about dreaming your heart out. You've read about going for it, about dreaming big, about pushing yourself further than you could have ever imagined. You've read about trusting God with your passions, about pursuing them with all that you have in you. You've read about disappointments and how sometimes plans fail but God doesn't leave your side. You've read about failures, heartache, closed doors. You've read about waiting and how God's timing is oftentimes nothing like yours. But most of all, you've read about *hope*. And you know what? That's where dreams start. From a place of hope. A hope that God is going to take your life and do more than you could have ever dreamed or imagined. In every dream you have and every path that dream takes you down, there is hope. There is hope in the waiting, there is hope in the disappointments, and there is hope in the joys and the successes. Find it. Hold onto it. And remember as you dream your heart out for the Lord that hope is always, *always* there.

> For I know the plans I have for you, says the Lord.
> They are plans for good and not for evil,
> to give you a future and a hope.
> JEREMIAH 29:11 TLB

> O Israel, hope in the LORD!
> For with the LORD there is steadfast love,
> and with him is plentiful redemption.
> PSALM 130:7 ESV

DAY 100

The Lord is all I have,
and so in Him I put my hope.
LAMENTATIONS 3:24 GNT

PRAYER

God, You have made me a dreamer.
You have given me the sweetest passions for life.
It is YOU whom I put my hope in.
It is YOU whom I will dream my heart out for.

Find these beautiful books, gifts,
and more on **dayspring.com**
as well as several retail stores near you.

ABOUT THE AUTHOR

Katy Fults, from Katygirl Designs, is a self-taught handletterer who is well-known for her beautifully drawn, affirming messages of God's hope, joy, and unconditional love. Through social media, women connect with Katy's everyday life as a busy wife, mom, and business owner. Her biggest passion in life is the Gospel and for others to know Jesus the way she knows Him.

You can find out more about DaySpring's Katygirl Collection, including books, journals, tumblers, plaques, and mugs all filled with sweet surprises of popping color and bold phrases, by visiting dayspring.com.

LIVE YOUR FAITH

Dear Friend,

This book was prayerfully crafted with you, the reader, in mind—every word, every sentence, every page—was thoughtfully written, designed, and packaged to encourage you...right where you are this very moment. At DaySpring, our vision is to see every person experience the life-changing message of God's love. So, as we worked through rough drafts, design changes, edits and details, we prayed for you to deeply experience His unfailing love, indescribable peace, and pure joy. It is our sincere hope that through these Truth-filled pages your heart will be blessed, knowing that God cares about you—your desires and disappointments, your challenges and dreams.

He knows. He cares. He loves you unconditionally.

BLESSINGS!
THE DAYSPRING BOOK TEAM

———————————

Additional copies of this book and
other DaySpring titles can be purchased
at fine bookstores everywhere.
Order online at dayspring.com
or
by phone at 1-877-751-4347